100

THINGS TO DO IN

ALBUQUERQUE

BEFORE YOU

DIE

Hiatt—
Enjoy the journey!
Ashley M Biggers

Ojito Wilderness

100

THINGS TO DO IN

ALBUQUERQUE
BEFORE YOU
DIE

3rd Edition

· ·

ASHLEY M. BIGGERS

REEDY PRESS

Library of Congress Control Number: 2022936999

ISBN: 9781681063768

Design by Jill Halpin

All photos by the author unless otherwise noted.

Printed in the United States of America
22 23 24 25 26   5 4 3 2 1

DEDICATION

To my son, Emmett. May you learn that in your hometown there's always something new to discover.

KiMo Theatre
Courtesy Library of Congress

CONTENTS

• • • • • • • • • • • • • • • • • • • •

Music and Entertainment

Sports and Recreation

Culture and History

Shopping and Fashion

PREFACE

I'm one of the rare Albuquerqueans who was born, raised, and lives in my hometown. I love that the Duke City—whether through the film industry, Sandia National Laboratories, Kirtland Air Force Base, University of New Mexico, or myriad other companies and institutions—beckons people from across the United States and the world. In some cases, these transplants explore more of the city than do locals. I've met many Albuquerqueans who comment that there's nothing to do here. I, for one, never have enough time for all the places I want to go and events I want to attend.

When I began writing the first edition of *100 Things to Do in Albuquerque Before You Die*, I wanted to capture all the enthralling aspects of the city I love, from the obvious picks to the offbeat ones. Yes, you'll find the Sandia Peak Tramway, Old Town, and the Isotopes in this guide, but it also includes the unexpected, quirky, and cultural places and happenings that make the Duke City such a dynamic place.

By the time I was penning this third edition, we were living in a new world: one where a global pandemic had reminded us all about the importance of home; impressed upon us the value of small, local businesses that are the heartbeat of our communities; and showed us that sometimes "adventuring" can mean trying something just out your front door. After these shared experiences, I hope you're inspired to travel in a way that reveals places, people, and cultures as only locals know them. And, if you're local, I hope this experience helps you rediscover a place you may think is out of ways to surprise you. I think you'll see Albuquerque still has a few things up its sleeves. These are unpredictable times, so, before you set out, it's best to check ahead with each destination regarding its operating hours and requirements for visiting.

This list isn't meant to be a ranking from first to worst. Instead, it's meant to be a collection of 100 things that will provide insight into Albuquerque—and inspire you to keep exploring.

If there are Albuquerque musts I haven't mentioned here, let me know on Facebook and Instagram at @ABQguide.

I hope your adventures are all good! Bueno, bye.

—Ashley M. Biggers

Indian Pueblo Cultural Center

Margarita at Sixty-Six Acres

FOOD AND DRINK

COMPLETE
THE BATTLE OF THE BURGERS

Green-chile cheeseburgers are to New Mexico as barbecue is to Texas. This down-home classic is synonymous with the state. Every local has his or her favorite burger joint, and there are many places that can lay claim to having the best of 'Burque's burgers. Some people prefer a greasy-spoon version; others opt for a gourmet version. Decide which you like best with this burger face-off: Laguna Burger vs. Holy Burger. The original Laguna Burger started west of Albuquerque at Laguna Pueblo's 66 Pit Stop. The pueblo later opened an in-town location serving a fast-food favorite: a thin patty topped with Hatch green chile, lettuce, tomato, cheese, red onion, pickle, and mustard. Holy Burger's upscale take has a toasted brioche bun piled high with a thick patty of New Mexico–grown beef, roasted green chile, cheddar cheese, and all the fixings. Add the pecan wood–smoked bacon for an extra burst of flavor.

Laguna Burger
2400 12th St. NW, (505) 352-8282, thelagunaburger.com

Holy Burger
700 Central Ave. SE, (505) 242-2991, holyburgernm.com

Neighborhood: North Valley and EDo, *Kid Friendly

TIP

Craving a vegetarian GCCB? The Acre serves a house-made beet/black bean/quinoa patty topped with green chile, red chile, cheddar cheese, and carrot bacon on a locally made green-chile bun with house-made French fries and pickles. theacrerestaurant.com

DRIZZLE HONEY ON A SOPAIPILLA
AT CASA DE BENAVIDEZ

Honey dripping down your fingers and arms is a sure sign you're enjoying Casa de Benavidez's sopaipillas—puffs of dough fried to crispy perfection that double as the state's unofficial dessert by concluding meals at New Mexican restaurants. Casa de Benavidez serves one of the best versions in the city. Paul and Rita Benavidez founded this North Valley eatery more than 50 years ago. The restaurant grew from a takeout business to a full-fledged restaurant that eventually overtook the family's rambling adobe home—thanks in no small part to their sopaipilla and popular sopaipilla burger. The restaurant, which offers serene patio dining beneath cottonwood trees during the summer, also serves savory versions stuffed with fajita meat, carne adovada, beef, beans, or chicharrones (fried pork rinds). Still, the classic sopaipilla slathered in honey can't be beat.

8032 4th St. NW, (505) 898-3311, casadebenavidez.com

Neighborhood: North Valley, *Kid Friendly

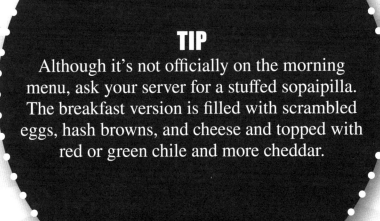

TIP

Although it's not officially on the morning menu, ask your server for a stuffed sopaipilla. The breakfast version is filled with scrambled eggs, hash browns, and cheese and topped with red or green chile and more cheddar.

DINE
AT FRENCHISH

Jennifer James is among a handful of star-worthy Albuquerque chefs. For seven consecutive years (2010–2016), the James Beard Foundation named her a semifinalist for its Best Chef: Southwest award; no other Albuquerque chef has been so honored to date. The awards are considered the culinary equivalent of the Oscars, and she certainly serves star-worthy dishes. She's overseen a handful of Duke City restaurants and, to follow her passion for French cuisine, she opened Frenchish in 2017 with Nelle Bauer. James isn't classically trained, so the "ish" gives her an out to take creative liberties. The open kitchen running the restaurant's breadth lets diners see their modern dishes take shape. James follows seasonality, so the menu shifts but may include appetizers like fried Brussels sprouts with beurre blanc sauce, beet tartar salad, or escargot prepared in puff pastry. Some dishes, like a pepper ice cream I ate during one meal, might challenge taste buds. But trust the chef. You'll be glad you did.

3509 Central Ave. NE, (505) 433-5911, frenchish.co

Neighborhood: Uptown

TIP
Reservations are always suggested, but there are usually seats available on short notice at the chef's counter or dessert bar.

SIP A MARGARITA
AT SIXTY-SIX ACRES

Some might call into question whether this "margarita" is the real deal. Why? Because it uses reposado agave spirit made in New Mexico rather than tequila, which must be made in that Mexican state to earn the name. But having a cocktail mixed with a homegrown spirit from Santa Fe's Tumbleroot distillery makes this version even better. The mixologists at Sixty-Six Acres blend the agave spirit with Naranja Orange Liqueur to give the Manzano Margarita just the right blend of sweet and sour. The restaurant's drink menu also features another margarita spinoff that pays homage to the character Skyler White, Walter White's wife in *Breaking Bad*, with white tequila and St-Germain (an elderflower liqueur) combined with lemon juice and lavender bitters. Pair your drink with any of the fantastic dishes at Sixty-Six Acres for a memorable meal or happy hour.

2400 12th St. NW, (505) 243-2230, sixtysixacres.com

Neighborhood: North Valley

TEAR OFF A PIECE
OF A FRONTIER SWEET ROLL

Frontier Restaurant has been an Albuquerque institution since it opened in 1971. The budget-friendly eatery serves ample plates to hungry college students from the University of New Mexico, which is just across Central Avenue. But postgraduate diners eat here, too, and locals have often voted it the best place for late-night eats and cheap eats. The barn-like restaurant is open from 5 a.m. to midnight, seven days a week, so you can order signature dishes such as green-chile stew nearly any time of day. The menu's apex, however, is the sweet roll, which was featured on the Travel Channel's *Man v. Food*. The pastry's cinnamon folds are coated with sugar and drenched with butter, making incredibly crave-worthy. Grab a table near a portrait of John Wayne (the owners have an affinity for the Duke) and enjoy. The rolls are also available at the four Golden Pride restaurants, which Larry and Dorothy Rainosek also own.

2400 Central Ave. SE, (505) 266-0550, frontierrestaurant.com

Neighborhood: University, *Kid Friendly

BREAKFAST
AT BARELAS COFFEE HOUSE

Barelas Coffee House has been a neighborhood institution for 40 years. Brothers James and Michael Gonzales opened the eatery in 1978, and their sister Benita Villanueva joined them quickly thereafter. Their family has lived in the Barelas neighborhood for four generations, and the restaurant is a testament to the family's longtime connections to the district where Spanish and Mexican families have lived for centuries. At Barelas Coffee House, servers know the names of every *vecino* (neighbor) and regular who enters the casual diner's doors. Movers and shakers meet here for out-of-the-office deal making, too. Local publications' readers' polls regularly acknowledge the dishes here as city favorites, including huevos rancheros deliciously smothered in chile and menudo (a traditional stew made with beef tripe).

1502 4th St. SW, (505) 843-7577, facebook.com/thebarelascoffeehouse

Neighborhood: Barelas, *Kid Friendly

PICK BERRIES
AT HEIDI'S RASPBERRY FARM

Heidi's raspberry jam—or, even better, raspberry red-chile jam—is a staple in Albuquerqueans' pantries. Founder Heidi Eleftheriou planted her first raspberry bushes in Corrales in 2000. With the plants overflowing, she began selling berries and jam at her flower stand at the Corrales Growers Market. The business blossomed and now operates out of a 3,000-square-foot warehouse space in Albuquerque's Brewery District to meet the multistate demand. In season, fresh berries are widely available at local farmers markets. However, there's little better than tasting the tart, luscious fruit straight from the hedges. After a brief hiatus, Eleftheriou welcomed visitors back to the Corrales farm in 2017 to pick their own raspberries and now blackberries. Visiting the field is a family-friendly outing, with toddlers ambling up and down the rows and older kids sneaking a few berries before they land in the pay-by-the-pint containers.

600 Andrews Ln., Corrales, (505) 898-1784, heidisraspberryfarm.com

Neighborhood: Corrales, *Kid Friendly

TIP

The harvest hits late August or September (depending on the weather). Check the farm's Facebook page or website for updates about season openings and berry availability. In recent years, the farm has requested visitors book time slots. They sell out a few weeks in advance.

DINE
AT INDIAN PUEBLO KITCHEN

Ensconced in the Indian Pueblo Cultural Center, this noteworthy restaurant is off the radar even for many locals. It should top lists, not fall off them. Chef Ray Naranjo—the first Native American chef in the restaurant's history—is helping new Native American cuisine gain a popular foothold by blending traditional Pueblo flavors into contemporary dishes. Brunch brings superfood waffles or griddle cakes packed with blue corn, amaranth, piñon, and pumpkin seeds. Dinner stars blue corn enchiladas with the Three Sisters (corn, beans, and squash). Don't miss the take-away Pueblo pies and oven-baked Pueblo cookies, just like you'd find if you ventured out to the state's 19 Pueblo communities. Check the restaurant's schedule for occasional intimate dining events when Naranjo prepare a multicourse tasting menu paired with wine. The menus often feature foraged ingredients and wild game. The dinners also include a Native cultural experience, such as dance or song performances, and artist demonstrations.

2401 12th St. NW, (505) 724-3510, puebloharvestcafe.com

Neighborhood: North Valley, *Kid Friendly

TIP

To increase your understanding of Pueblo agriculture and culinary traditions, tour the cultural center's Resilience Garden—a plot using traditional Pueblo farming methods— growing across the parking lot from Indian Pueblo Kitchen.

SIP BUBBLY
FROM GRUET

Although wine is now produced in all 50 states, no others can claim this accolade: New Mexico produced wine before any other region in the country—yes, even before California. Franciscan monks planted the first mission grapevines here in 1629, south of Albuquerque. Today Duke City–area vintners stick to varietals more pleasing to the contemporary palate. Founded in 1984 by Gilbert Gruet and overseen by the family, Gruet Winery is one of the state's marquee vintners. Gruet is internationally known for its pinot noir and chardonnay–based méthode champenoise sparkling wines. The label has earned numerous awards. In 2011, *Wine Spectator* named the Gruet NV Blanc de Noirs a top 100 wine in the world. Gruet also produces still wines, including the noteworthy rosé created in partnership with Tamaya Vineyard. Owned by Santa Ana Pueblo, Tamaya Vineyard is one of the only Native American–owned commercial vineyards in the country and the only one grown from scratch by a tribe.

Tasting Room
8400 Pan American Fwy. NE, (505) 821-0055, gruetwinery.com

Neighborhood: Northeast Heights

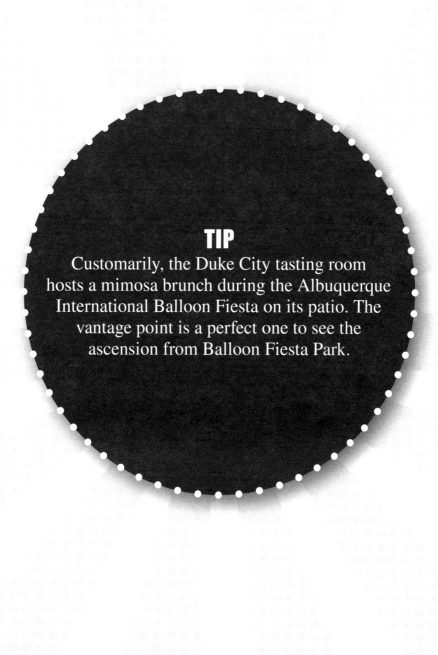

TIP

Customarily, the Duke City tasting room hosts a mimosa brunch during the Albuquerque International Balloon Fiesta on its patio. The vantage point is a perfect one to see the ascension from Balloon Fiesta Park.

NIBBLE A BISCOCHITO
AT GOLDEN CROWN PANADERIA

New Mexico's official state cookie, the biscochito, is an anise-flavored, cinnamon-sugar number traditionally served at Christmas. Golden Crown Panaderia makes some 2,500 dozen each holiday season, but the Old Town–neighborhood bakery makes them by hand year-round. Pratt Morales opened the bakery in 1972; today, he runs it with his son, Chris, who grew up baking alongside his father. When you walk into the adobe building bedecked with murals of hollyhocks, a server will hand you a crumbly biscochito to eat while you're sifting through the array of treats on the menu. Choose between traditional, chocolate, and cappuccino versions. For a gluten-free option, choose the blue-corn version. Golden Crown also serves sweet and savory empanadas, spicy green-chile bread, and made-to-order pizzas. Pratt also shapes turkey-shaped loaves pretty enough for a holiday table centerpiece.

1103 Mountain Rd. NW, (505) 243-2424, goldencrown.biz

Neighborhood: Old Town, *Kid Friendly

TOAST THE CITY
FROM LEVEL 5

Hotel Chaco, the first newly built hotel near Old Town in decades, has become a go-to spot for its rooftop restaurant and lounge. Hotel designers drew inspiration from the great houses now protected as Chaco Culture National Historical Park for the building's atmosphere and finishes, including the height of the hotel at five stories. The designers wanted visitors to have a similar vantage as that of the great houses. From the swanky hotel's fifth-story roost, diners can take in panoramic views of the Sandia Mountains, Old Town, and downtown. During October's Albuquerque International Balloon Fiesta, it's also a prime balloon-viewing perch. The food menu has global appeal but it is dusted with indigenous ingredients such as Anasazi beans and calabacitas (corn, squash, and chile). The beverage menu leans into local wine and beer.

2000 Bellamah Ave. NW, (505) 318-3998, hotelchaco.com

Neighborhood: Sawmill District

BITE
INTO BUFFETT'S CANDIES

Albuquerqueans go nuts—pardon the pun—for the piñon candies at Buffett's. Founder George Buffett's mother encouraged him to start a candy business because all he needed was "just a pot and a stove." After spending confectioner's busy season (Halloween to Easter) working for Los Angeles–based See's Candy, he founded the shop in 1956. George's children, Patty, George II, and John, still run the business in its original location today. After more than 60 years, the towering candy-cane sculpture outside the shop has become a landmark. For sweet-toothed locals and visitors it points the way to nut confections (including toffee, truffles, pralines, and brittles) made with the small buttery piñons native to New Mexico, as well as other sweet treats. The Duke City mainstay has been featured on *Delicious Destinations*, hosted by Andrew Zimmern on the Travel Channel.

7001 Lomas Blvd. NE, (505) 265-7731, buffettscandies.com

Neighborhood: Uptown, *Kid Friendly

TASTE
RIO GRANDE CUISINE
AT CAMPO

Los Poblanos Historic Inn and Organic Farm has a deep agricultural history that begins when Native Americans, then Spanish and Mexican settlers, farmed fertile fields here. Today, Los Poblanos operates a cultural center designed by iconic Southwest architect John Gaw Meem, a 50-room inn, a farm shop, and, of course, the restaurant. Native New Mexican and six-time James Beard Award–finalist chef Jonathan Perno helms the eatery as executive chef. He works with the property's stewards, the Rembe family, to craft Rio Grande cuisine that's both rugged and refined. At Campo, which is housed in renovated dairy barn overlooking lavender fields, Campo sings with local, seasonal ingredients. The chefs and farmers at Los Poblanos work hand in hand to grow heirloom and native landrace crops, including resurrecting crops that have nearly been lost or fallen out of favor.

4803 Rio Grande Blvd. NW, (505) 338-1615, lospoblanos.com

Neighborhood: Los Ranchos de Albuquerque

DINE IN THE FIELD
AT FARM & TABLE

When residential development threatened to overtake yet more North Valley farm fields, Cheri Montoya's father, David, snapped up the fertile land on which Farm & Table now sits. Montoya launched Farm & Table to preserve the Rio Grande Valley's agricultural heritage. Diners sitting inside the intimate restaurant or on its patio (the place to be on summer nights) can see acreage where much of their dinner is grown. At the time of this writing, the farm is transitioning to a permaculture farm, which emphasizes whole system thinking and integrates decorative landscaping with agricultural production in the name of sustainability. When ingredients can't come from the resident farm, the chef gathers them from a slew of local farmers and purveyors. The New American dishes let ingredients shine. Although menus shift with the seasons, previous editions have highlighted pan-seared rainbow trout with greens and poblano crema, and winter squash ravioli with mushroom and piñon. Don't miss the restaurant's eclectic global wine list.

8917 4th St. NW, (505) 503-7124, farmandtablenm.com

Neighborhood: North Valley, *Kid Friendly

TIP

Farm & Table is set in a quaint adobe with limited seating. Be sure to make a reservation, particularly on weekend evenings and special occasions. Check the restaurant's calendar for wine dinners and yoga and meditation sessions.

SAVOR
MR. POWDRELL'S BARBEQUE

Mr. Powdrell's Barbeque has been a Duke City staple since the late Pete Powdrell opened his North Valley restaurant in 1962. The restaurant uses family recipes that began with Pete's great-grandfather, Isaac, who invented a tangy barbecue sauce and perfected his own technique for slow-smoking meats over an open pit with hickory wood in Baton Rouge, Louisiana. Pete packed up these family recipes, his wife, and eleven children and migrated to New Mexico via Texas in 1958. According to family lore, he arrived with little more than his barbecue knowhow and entrepreneurial spirit. His hard work created a barbecue dynasty in the Duke City, which his family has now carried on for more than than 60 years by serving tasty pork, beef, and chicken, as well as noteworthy desserts such as sweet potato pie and peach cobbler.

Original location
5209 4th St. NW, (505) 345-8086

Central
11301 Central Ave. NE, (505) 298-6766

bbqandsoulfoodabq.com

Neighborhood: North Valley, *Kid Friendly

BRUNCH
AT THE GROVE CAFE & MARKET

This eatery is fresh—from the local, seasonal ingredients to the bright, light-filled setting. Jason and Lauren Greene have operated the bustling restaurant since 2006, serving salads, sandwiches, and breakfast items made from New Mexican produce, all-natural meats, and artisan breads and cheeses. For weekend brunch, it's prime mimosa-sipping territory. Don't miss the Grove pancakes—which are like French crepes topped with fresh fruit, creme fraiche, and local honey—and the pillowy English muffins. If you lean toward lunch, try the Farmers Salad, with golden beets, Marcona almonds, and goat cheese, or the Turkey Toastie sandwich, with Havarti cheese pressed on whole-wheat bread. Although most customers love the colorful macarons and cupcakes, for my money, the brown butter bourbon butterscotch cookie is the best around.

600 Central Ave. SE, (505) 248-9800, thegrovecafemarket.com

Neighborhood: EDo, *Kid Friendly

TIP

Breaking Bad fans will remember this eatery as the setting where Walter White (Bryan Cranston) laced a packet of stevia with ricin poison to kill his former business partner Lydia Rodarte-Quayle (Laura Fraser). The restaurant stocks packets of stevia at the coffee stand, but they're perfectly safe.

GRAB A TABLE ON THE PATIO
AT EL PINTO RESTAURANT

Burqueños can debate the best New Mexican food in town until, well, it's time for the next meal. El Pinto is usually in the running for its menu, which overflows with a tasty complement of classic New Mexican dishes. The restaurant's atmosphere helps it arrive at the front of the pack. Its set in a quintessentially New Mexican hacienda with sprawling rooms and grand portals. If the weather's nice, request a table outside beneath hundred-year-old cottonwood trees, where the strains of mariachi music often rise above conversations shared over margaritas on the rocks. Members of the Thomas family have been serving their family recipes at El Pinto, or "the spot," since 1962. Most recently, twin brothers Jim and John have been at the helm. The duo also began jarring the restaurant's signature salsa.

10500 4th St. NW, (505) 898-1771, elpinto.com

Neighborhood: North Valley, *Kid Friendly

TIP

The Tequila Bar at El Pinto stocks 160 tequilas. Although you might be tempted into a margarita—and who wouldn't be with the "Salsa Twins" favorite pick that features specially produced Barrel Select Añejo, Cointreau, simple syrup, and fresh squeezed lime?—the best way to experience the selection is with a tasting flight featuring three sipping (not shooting) tequilas and a palate cleanser.

CYCLE 'ROUND
TO BIKE IN COFFEE

Albuquerque has a bevy of excellent coffee shops, but none offer the atmosphere of Bike In Coffee, located at Old Town Farm. It welcomes visitors Thursday through Sunday mornings to a food stand. There's just one catch: you must arrive by pedal power. To preserve the farm's idyllic setting—and their relationship with neighbors—owners Lanny Tonning and Linda Thorne ask visitors to cycle to the farm. Founded in 1977, Old Town Farm's gardens have slowly been taking over horse corrals with some 300 varieties of produce. After they tired of trucking produce to farmers markets, they invited customers to come to them instead. Diners order at the counter, then pick a spot on the wraparound porch or in the garden to enjoy their meal. It's hard to know what to choose: crepes, fruit pastries using the farm's raspberries or jujubes, breakfast burritos, or tacos. Weather shutters the shop from mid-December to early February, so check for closures during this period.

949 Montoya St. NW, (505) 764-9116, oldtownfarm.com

Neighborhood: Old Town, *Kid Friendly

TIP

The farm sits at the nexus of the I-40 bike trail, the Paseo del Bosque Trail, Mountain Road (a bicycle boulevard where the speed limit for car traffic is 18 miles per hour), and sleepy Montoya Street, providing a variety of routes to follow to the farm. Have a flat? Bici-Fixx mobile bike shop will help you fix it on Saturdays.

SIT AT THE COUNTER
AT DURAN CENTRAL PHARMACY

This working pharmacy doubles as a New Mexican restaurant. Pete Duran founded his eponymous pharmacy in 1942. Upon his retirement in 1965, he sold the business to his staff pharmacist Robert Ghattas. Ghattas moved the business to its present location in 1975, where it soon included a soda fountain. The business has stayed in the Ghattas family—Robert's daughter Mona carries on the business today—as it has expanded. The vintage soda fountain stayed, but it outgrew malts and milkshakes to become a full-fledged restaurant serving enchiladas, burritos, and must-try tortilla burgers. The New Mexican favorites are smothered in good-enough-to-jar red or green chile (grab one to take home with you). One of the best things on the menu, however, is a simple basketball-sized, hand-rolled tortilla slathered in butter.

1815 Central Ave. NW, (505) 247-4141, duransrx.com

Neighborhood: West Downtown

TIP
If you're hankering for a caffeine jolt, Duran shares a building with Remedy Coffee. remedycoffeeabq.com

PLACE YOUR ORDER
AT A SHIPPING CONTAINER PARK

New Mexico's first shipping-container park, Green Jeans Farmery, quickly became one of Albuquerque's favorite food spots. In 2020, its sister park, Tin Can Alley, joined the food hall fleet. Both are next-level takes on the food court with a trove of local restaurants operating out of the double-decker containers. Every member of your party can order something different at these eateries. Santa Fe Brewing Company—the state's original craft brewery—anchors both locations. Amore Neapolitan, serving some of the best pizza in town; Squeezed Juice Bar, offering cold-pressed juice; Nitro Fog Creamery, scooping made-to-order ice cream; and Pho Kup, dishing out fresh Vietnamese cuisine, are staples at both food halls. Tin Can Alley's design allows for ample indoor seating. Green Jeans is most popular in the summer, thanks to its open-air approach, but there's indoor seating, too, so don't cross it off your list come winter.

Green Jeans Farmery
3600 Cutler Ave. NE, (505) 313-0042, greenjeansfarmery.com

Tin Can Alley
6110 Alameda Blvd. NE, (505) 208-0508, tincanalleyabq.com

Neighborhood: Midtown, *Kid Friendly

GRAB A SLICE
AT RESTORATION PIZZA

Eat pizza. Drink beer. It seems like a simple formula, but there's more to this eatery than meets the eye. The leadership team of Bosque Brewery, which also owns Restoration Pizza, wanted their business to give back. They created a diverse, inclusive working environment where underemployed individuals have stable, well-paid work. To find employees, the pizza joint collaborates with agencies such as New Mexico Commission for the Blind; Ability First, a nonprofit caring for adults with disabilities; and ARCA, a nonprofit serving individuals with intellectual, developmental, and cognitive disabilities. The teamwork doesn't stop there. They continue to work with the partner organizations to make sure that newly hired staff members can stick around. They help with challenges that typically keep these individuals out of work, such as transportation.

5161 Lang Ave. NE, Ste. A, (505) 582-2720, restorationpizza.com

Neighborhood: Northeast Heights, *Kid Friendly

PEDAL
TO LOCAL BREWERIES

Albuquerque has dozens of craft breweries and more open each month. It has even ranked as high as 12th in the US for breweries per capita. With that many suds shops in the running, it could take weeks to try them all, but you can get a solid flight during a Bike & Brew Tour with Routes Bicycle Tours. During the tour, you'll pedal to three or more taprooms, including the likes of Canteen Brewhouse, Marble Brewery, Bosque Brewing Company, Santa Fe Brewing Company, and Sidetrack Brewing Company, to sample a dozen styles of beer. This hoppy-hour tour is just one of Routes' many themed outings, which also include wine-, taco-, and chile-centric offerings, as well as sightseeing tours. The company rents bikes for those hoping to venture out independently.

2113 Charlevoix St. NW, (505) 933-5667, routesrentals.com

Neighborhood: Old Town

TASTE A TAMALE
FROM VEGOS

Vegos owner/chef, Elizabeth Bibiano, is a pro at adapting New Mexican dishes into vegan-friendly fare. Vegos's signature tamale uses red-chile jackfruit as a stand-in for pork. The tropical tree fruit has become a popular meat substitute. When cooked, it can take on the flaky texture of slow-cooked pork. Vegos's creation is a look-a-like-tamale with enough flavor to make your abuela proud. "They're tamales like grandma would make," she says. "People were amazed they didn't have meat in them. It let me show people you can still enjoy flavor and culture while being plant-based." Vegos began as a food truck and grew into a brick-and-mortar shop serving a full menu of burritos and comfort foods, such as a fried "chicken" sandwiches (made using tofu). The hearty dishes are tasty enough to please meat-eaters, too.

4003 Carlisle Blvd. NE, (505) 554-1041, vegosabq.com

Neighborhood: Northeast Heights, *Kid Friendly

TIP

If you're looking for a traditional tamale, El Modelo Mexican Foods has been serving a stellar version since 1929. Carmen Garcia founded the restaurant in a three-room home, where she'd rise every day at 2 a.m. to make tortillas by hand to sell. The budding entrepreneur hired Petra Vargas to make tamales. She eventually taught the whole family to make the signature dish and helped the business grow out of the home and into its Barelas location. elmodelomexicanfoods.com

---

SAMPLE THE SMORGASBORD
AT SAWMILL MARKET

New Mexico's first food hall features two dozen locally owned and operated food stands. The market took over the former home of Paxton Lumber Company. The "Home of Beautiful Woods" stood in the industrial Sawmill District for decades, but it shuttered in 1999. In 2018, boutique hotel and hospitality company Heritage Hotels & Resorts purchased the building and began reimagining it. The food hall officially opened in 2020 just before the pandemic. After that false start, the food hall is thriving with a diverse array of culinary concepts from emerging and experienced restauranteurs. The lineup changes periodically, but you can expect to find palate-pleasing plates of New Mexican, Asian, and other global foods, as well as coffee, cocktails, and craft beer.

1909 Bellamah Ave. NW, (505) 563-4473, sawmillmarket.com

Neighborhood: Sawmill, *Kid Friendly

KiMo Theatre

MUSIC
AND ENTERTAINMENT

GROOVE
AT ¡GLOBALQUERQUE!

There are few festivals in the US where world music greats such as Calypso Rose and the Afro-Cuban All Stars play in the same time slot. (Calypso Rose is a prolific writer and songstress, most popularly of calypso music. The Afro-Cuban All Stars recorded the legendary *Buena Vista Social Club* album and are noted for reviving classic Cuban son music.) These headliners may have hit the stage just one year at ¡Globalquerque!, but stars such as these are the norm, not the exception, at the two-day festival held almost every September since 2005. Since that year, ¡Globalquerque! has featured artists from 75 countries and across the US. Most play cultural-roots music, often not in English, but that language barrier doesn't keep audiences from grooving at the National Hispanic Cultural Center, where the celebration is currently held. "World music is where the adventure is right now," says founder Tom Frouge. It's a major regional music fest that shouldn't be missed.

National Hispanic Cultural Center
1701 4th St. SW, (505) 246-2261, globalquerque.org

Neighborhood: Barelas

ATTEND AN EVENT
AT KIMO THEATRE

The KiMo Theatre is one of Albuquerque's most prominent architectural landmarks, but it's certainly no relic: the KiMo's schedule teems with events. Now listed on the National Register of Historic Places, the picture palace and vaudeville theater opened in 1927. Today, it screens films, hosts literary talks, and presents folk music concerts beneath its proscenium arch. The building's distinctive design elements are as notable as what happens on stage. Entrepreneur Oreste Bachechi hired Carl Boller, of the Boller Brothers, to design what became the theater's hallmark style. It fused Southwestern and Art Moderne influences into Pueblo Deco style. Upon its opening, Pablo Abeita, then governor of Isleta Pueblo, named the theater using a combination of two Tewa words translated as "king of its kind." The theater became dilapidated in the 1960s, but the City of Albuquerque later purchased and renovated the structure.

421 Central Ave. NW, (505) 768-3522, kimotickets.com

Neighborhood: Downtown, *Kid Friendly (depending on the presentation)

DISCOVER
WHAT THE CHATTER IS ABOUT

French composer Claude Debussy once remarked that "works of art make rules; rules do not make works of art." Chatter is the rule breaker—and maker—of Albuquerque classical music. Chatter presents Sunday concerts 50 weeks a year with iconic and contemporary classical works accompanied by spoken-word poetry and a two-minute celebration of silence. David Felberg, still artistic director, and friend Eric Walters founded Chatter in 2002 to gain conducting and composing experience. Chatter merged with the Church of Beethoven, the first organization to make Sunday concerts a city tradition, in 2010. Previous performances have included works by Bach and Chopin as well as compositions by modern composers that challenge even its sophisticated audience's ears. Arrive early to purchase a cappuccino and partake of the breakfast pastries Chatter volunteers prepare.

912 3rd St. NW, chatterabq.org

Neighborhood: Wells Park

TIP

Each year, Chatter also presents six or so cabarets—chamber music performances in intimate settings with wine/beer and appetizers—and a couple of large-scale concerts. In the past, the locations for those concerts have included the Albuquerque Rail Yards and Albuquerque Museum.

GET SPICY
AT NATIONAL FIERY FOODS AND BARBECUE SHOW

Burqueños like chile on just about everything, and this festival celebrates the peppers' many varieties and incarnations. Founded in 1988 by author Dave DeWitt, a.k.a. "the Pope of Peppers," the National Fiery Foods and Barbecue Show is the spiciest show of its kind in the world. During the three-day March event, some 200 vendors sponsor booths, most offering tastes of food products. If you want to incite a bout between your taste buds and some of the hottest products on the Scoville heat scale this is your kind of event. I once overheard an attendee remark, quite delightedly, about a sample, "This feels like it's melting my insides!" Not all products are scorching, however. The food show also grants Scovie Awards to the best-tasting seasonings, marinades, and condiments. Grab a program so you can navigate to award winners. The show also includes chef demonstrations from greats who can bring the heat.

fieryfoodsshow.com

Neighborhood: Northeast Heights

LEVEL UP
AT ELECTRIC PLAYHOUSE

Visiting Electric Playhouse feels like playing a life-sized video game. Here, digital projectors and motion-tracking software create interactive games and art installations. In the immersive Kaleidatorium, players compete to step on the most colored squares on the ground. In the Arena, gamers face off in an enormous air hockey game shooting digitally projected spheres from one end of the room to the next with their bodies directing the pucks. And in the Courts, they compete in a gigantic version of dodgeball. In smaller pods, visitors use motions to splatter digital paint, build mandalas, and create other artistic designs. These are just a few examples of the ever-changing lineup of family-friendly games and displays inside the digital-recreation wonderland. The space opened in 2020 and has since built a following not only for its games but also for special events such as interactive-themed dining experiences.

5201 Ouray Rd. NW, (505) 832-7562, electricplayhouse.com

Neighborhood: Westside, *Kid Friendly

FIND A SPOT
IN THE GRASS
FOR ZOO NIGHTS

Pack a picnic, grab the kids, and throw out a blanket on the lawn at the ABQ BioPark Zoo for the Zoo Nights concert series. The likes of the Indigo Girls and Chris Isaak have played in the band shell, as have touring acts in pop-rock, Americana, folk, Latin, and jazz. You can pack your own picnic or grab food from the zoo's own Cottonwood Cafe or a variety of snack bars. Be sure to arrive early on select summer Saturdays, when the concerts are held, to explore the 64-acre zoo. All of the exhibits are open except Penguin Chill. Many of the animals are active at dusk; occasionally, you'll hear the lions roaring in the background of concerts.

903 10th St. SW, (505) 768-2000, cabq.gov

Neighborhood: South Valley, *Kid Friendly

TIP

The ABQ BioPark Botanic Garden also hosts a series of summer concerts, Garden Sounds, which often features local acts.

SEE A PLAY
AT ALBUQUERQUE LITTLE THEATRE

The Albuquerque Little Theatre may be the oldest community theater group in the city, but its annual season of shows is fresh and lively. The seasons often include local productions of Broadway theatrical and musical hits, like *A Christmas Carol* and *Mamma Mia!*, and shows staged with families in mind, like *Shrek the Musical*. Founded in 1930, the Albuquerque Little Theatre passed a half dozen years at the KiMo Theatre before moving into its current home in 1936. Renowned architect John Gaw Meem designed the building and the Works Progress Administration built it. The likes of Vivian Vance, who played Ethel Mertz on *I Love Lucy*; Don Knotts, of the *Andy Griffith Show* and *Three's Company*; and Bill Daily, of *I Dream of Jeannie*, have graced this historic stage.

224 San Pasquale Ave. SW, (505) 242-4750, albuquerquelittletheatre.org

Neighborhood: Old Town, *Kid Friendly (depending on the show)

TIP
Albuquerque's theater scene is dynamic, particularly for a city of its size. To learn more about Albuquerque's more than 40 theater companies and venues, visit abqtheatre.org.

GET YOUR KICKS
AT ROUTE 66 SUMMERFEST

There are a few happenings that bring Albuquerqueans out in force. This block party is one of them. Central Avenue, a.k.a. "old Route 66," closes to regular car traffic from Girard Boulevard to Washington Street for this summer celebration. Several blocks of Nob Hill bustle with food vendors, artisan and crafts booths, local beer and wine gardens, a kids' zone with free activities, and live music stages. Traditionally, a nationally headlining act takes center stage. Nob Hill shops and restaurants lining Central also throw open their doors for the festivities. The event recalls Route 66's halcyon days with a classic car show and a burnout competition (where drivers smoke their rear tires to leave rubber streaks on the pavement).

cabq.gov

Neighborhood: Nob Hill, *Kid Friendly

TIP
Traffic can be a beast, so check for park-and-ride options before you go.

● ●

LISTEN TO LIVE MUSIC
AT LOBO THEATER

The Lobo Theater's first act began in 1938 when it debuted as a movie theater. Over the years, it continued that focus by screening second-run, European, and indie flicks. Those operations ended in 2000 when it began moonlighting as a venue for churches. The pandemic closed the curtain on those operations as well. That's when it came to the attention of J. Richard Rivas, managing broker of Commercial Real Estate Services. When his search for the right tenant came up empty, he decided to lease and renovate the space himself, which he did. It reopened in October 2021 as a live-music and special-event venue as well as a swanky, 1940s-style lounge where visitors can sip cocktails and enjoy food from nearby restaurants. The 300-seat concert hall also leaves a bit of room to dance, so don't resist the urge if the mood strikes you.

3013 Central Ave. NE, loboabq.com

Neighborhood: Nob Hill

RIFF
AT OUTPOST PERFORMANCE SPACE

This no-frills concert venue is all about the music. Both a nonprofit organization and an intimate performance space, the Outpost presents more than 100 shows per year (when at full force). National Endowment for the Arts Jazz Masters—winners of the most prestigious award conferred on such musicians—perform here frequently, including during the summer New Mexico Jazz Festival. Summer also brings an all-local jazz series featuring Dixie to bop. You'll hear other genres here, too, including folk, blues, and experimental music. Depending on the concert, the space may be set up like a jazz lounge or a concert hall. Either way, the 160-seat house is an intimate venue where you can see musicians at their formidable bests. Outpost also hangs visual arts shows—usually to tie into performances—and hosts spoken-word poetry slams and amateur nights where locals can get their starts.

210 Yale Blvd. SE, (505) 268-0044, outpostspace.org

Neighborhood: University

TIP
Paid parking is available alongside the building or across the street. Seating is first come, first served, so arrive early to find a good vantage point.

DRAW ANOTHER CARD
AT EMPIRE BOARD GAME LIBRARY

Take family game night to the next level at this Nob Hill shop, which stocks more than 850 board and card games for guests to play. Opened in April 2015, this board game café has a family-friendly vibe in a neighborhood otherwise known for its shopping, dining, and nightlife. Longtime neighborhood resident Rory Veronda envisioned a place to gather sans alcohol when founding the game library. Instead, gamers gather around cups of locally roasted coffee and both classic and new board games when they play their choice of the library's games by the hour. If the selection seems overwhelming, shop game masters can suggest the best ones for your group, and—perhaps even better—they can quickly demonstrate how to play so you can spend less time memorizing the rule book and longer absorbed in play.

3503 Central Ave. NE, (505) 232-4263, empiregamelibrary.com

Neighborhood: Nob Hill, *Kid Friendly

SEE A SHOW
AT POPEJOY HALL

Broadway comes to New Mexico at Popejoy Hall, the biggest indoor performance hall in the state—and an elegant one, too. This University of New Mexico venue hosts touring productions of *Wicked*, the *Book of Mormon*, and other hits. But its lineup includes more than Broadway shows. Audience members pack the 1,985-seat theater to hear speakers such as David Sedaris and Ira Glass and to see Las Vegas headliner the Blue Man Group and New York export the Martha Graham Dance Company. Homegrown groups take the stage here as well, including the New Mexico Philharmonic. The performance hall opened in 1966 and is named after former University of New Mexico president Tom Popejoy, who spent nearly 20 years convincing stakeholders that the campus should have a dedicated performing arts venue. The theater continues to evolve as additions and restorations amplify the experience.

Redondo Drive and Stanford Drive (at the University of New Mexico Center for the Arts), (505) 277-9771, popejoypresents.com

Tickets: (505) 925-5858, (877) 664-8661, unmtickets.com

Neighborhood: University, *Kid Friendly (depending on the show)

Albuquerque International Balloon Fiesta

SPORTS AND RECREATION

THRU-BIKE OR HIKE
THE PASEO DEL BOSQUE TRAIL

The Paseo del Bosque Trail has earned a first-place finish in the hearts of Albuquerque's cyclists and runners as the city's premier multi-use path. The 16-mile trail runs between the city's north and south edges uninterrupted by car traffic and through the scenic Rio Grande bosque (forest). If you complete its entire length, you'll spot elephants, whose ABQ BioPark Zoo enclosure is visible from the path; public art at Tingley Beach; the Rio Grande Nature Center State Park; and Canada geese at the Valle de Oro National Wildlife Refuge, the city's 570-acre urban bird sanctuary. There are access points (and often parking areas) at Alameda Boulevard, Paseo del Norte Boulevard, Montano Road, Campbell Road, Central Avenue, Marquez Street, and Rio Bravo Boulevard.

(505) 452-5200, cabq.gov/parksandrecreation/open-space/lands/
paseo-del-bosque-trail

Neighborhoods: South Valley to North Valley, *Kid Friendly

PADDLE
THE RIO GRANDE

Albuquerque and water sports go together like peanut butter and bananas—unexpected, perhaps, but delightful. The Rio Grande, the fourth-longest river in the US, cuts a sinuous path through the city's heart, much to the delight of paddle-sport enthusiasts. Kayaks and paddleboards, which sit high in the water, fare well in the sometimes-shallow waters that flow through this stretch of river. The low-and-slow waters are friendly to beginners or inexperienced paddlers, so first-timers and families shouldn't hesitate to take an outing. Coasting along the placid waters, paddlers can see geese, coyotes, and beavers that come to float, drink, and dip in the Rio Grande. Its feels like an oasis in the center of the urban landscape.

Neighborhood: Citywide, *Kid Friendly

TIP

Albuquerque's Mountain Stream & Trail Adventures offers kayak and paddle board rentals. mstadventures.com

---

STROLL
THE RIO GRANDE
NATURE CENTER STATE PARK

Walking the riverside trails through the cottonwood forests at the Rio Grande Nature Center State Park, you can scarcely tell you're in the heart of a metropolitan area. One of New Mexico's 35 state parks, it preserves 270 acres of cottonwood stands, wetlands, and meadows along the Rio Grande Flyway, making it a year-round destination for birders. More than 250 species have been sighted here, including sandhill cranes, bald eagles, and great blue herons. You can view waterfowl at the Candelaria Wetlands and the Discovery Pond. Three easy nature trails also await: the Riverwalk Trail, a one-mile loop along the river; the Bosque Loop Trail, a 0.8-mile trail; and the Aldo Leopold Trail, which is dedicated to the grandfather of the conservation movement and leads to the Aldo Leopold Forest. Throughout the year, you may encounter beavers, cottontail rabbits, or coyotes.

2901 Candelaria NW, (505) 344-7240, rgnc.org, nmparks.com

Neighborhood: North Valley, *Kid Friendly

TIP
The volunteer Friends of the Rio Grande Nature Center offer guided weekend bird walks, nature walks, and monthly twilight hikes. Check the schedule online to join.

WALK
THE WIDE-OPEN SPACE

Albuquerque has more parkland per capita than any other city in the US. That's in large part thanks to the City of Albuquerque, which owns more than 27,000 acres in 27 tracts. The Open Space Visitor Center is a fitting jumping-off point for your explorations. The center has interpretive exhibits, an art gallery, and agricultural fields that draw an array of wildlife. To get out on the Open Space trails, locals favor Elena Gallegos Picnic Area and Albert G. Simms Park in the foothills of the Sandia Mountains. A network of paths loops through the 640-acre park, wending through stands of piñon and juniper and unfolding into views of the Sandias (to the east), Mount Taylor (to the west), and the Jemez Mountains (to the north). From here, the trail network extends into Sandia Mountain Wilderness.

Visitor Center
6500 Coors Blvd. NW, (505) 897-8831, cabq.gov

Neighborhood: Citywide, *Kid Friendly

WING YOUR WAY
TO VALLE DE ORO NATIONAL
WILDLIFE REFUGE

In 2013, Valle de Oro became the first urban wildlife refuge in the Southwest. Several years after official protection of the 570-acre plot in the South Valley, it still takes some imagination to visualize the land's transformation from its previous life as the Price Dairy Valle Gold Farms into the planned reserve. Proposals include reintroducing rolling topography, wetlands, salt grass meadows, and protecting existing cottonwood forest. Already frequented by several hundred species of avian and mammalian wildlife, these features will further benefit and attract fauna to the oasis within the largely industrial and agricultural neighborhood. Visitors are welcome to wander the fields and walk along the sandy paths of the Rio Grande daily from 6 a.m. to 6 p.m. to observe the prairie dogs, hawks, and coyotes (among many other species) here. A newly built visitor center offers guidance to trek the four nature trails, which range in distance from .25 to 1.5 miles.

7851 2nd St. SW, (505) 248-6667, fws.gov/refuge/valle_de_oro

Neighborhood: South Valley, *Kid Friendly

JOIN
THE BLACK AND YELLOW FAMILIA

New Mexico United has rallied fans since the United Soccer League (USL) team was announced in 2018. They kicked off their inaugural season on March 9, 2019, in front of a hometown crowd at Isotopes Park (a.k.a. "the Lab") and went on to set multiple records their first year with their historic run at the US Open Cup and a place atop the USL's leaderboard for average fan attendance. While attending a home game, you'll quickly be pulled into the incredible energy of thousands of fans cheering and waving flags through a yellow haze (courtesy of the smoke bombs released after goals). That crowd support has attracted players to join the United—and made the Lab a fearsome environment for the team's rivals. United has qualified for the USL championship playoffs multiple times, but to its legions of fans, the team means more than what happens on the pitch during the March–October season. With this team, the philosophy of "Somos Unidos!" (We Are United!) runs deep.

newmexicoutd.com

Isotopes Park
1601 Avenida Cesar Chavez SE

Neighborhood: University, *Kid Friendly

FLY
IN A HOT-AIR BALLOON

It may be a lofty goal—for yourself and your budget—but getting up, up, and away in a hot-air balloon deserves a spot on your Duke City bucket list. The entire experience is thrilling, from watching the envelope inflate and stand, to stepping inside the reinforced basket, to effortlessly lifting off. The flight experience feels like magic. The balloon floats nearly soundlessly (except for the burner firing loudly) through the city's signature blue skies. Down below, you can see the world carrying on, yet it all feels so far away. Landing can be a bit bumpy, but well worth the experience. First-timers often toast with champagne when their flights end. Although many rides take place during the Albuquerque International Balloon Fiesta, they are available year-round. Only wind or the occasional storm grounds flights.

Rainbow Ryders Hot Air Balloon Co.
5601 Eagle Rock Ave. NE, (505) 823-1111, rainbowryders.com

CLIMB
LA LUZ TRAIL

Trekking La Luz Trail is a rite of passage for Albuquerqueans. The eight-mile trail (one way) climbs 4,000 feet from the foothills to the Sandia Mountains crest. Switchbacks manage the steep trail's ascent through piñon and juniper-dotted foothills to ponderosa forests. Views of the city and the Rio Grande Valley below are worth the sweat. Once you've summited, you can descend the way you came or traipse over to the Sandia Peak Tramway departure area to glide back to the base (which, take note, will drop you off in a different parking lot than the one you started in). This is a strenuous trail; only those with the physical fitness to accomplish the hike should attempt it. Visitors should take note that the trail's altitude ranges from 7,000 to more than 10,000 feet, and there's dramatically different weather on the peak than at the base.

Cibola National Forest Sandia Ranger Station
(505) 281-3304, fs.usda.gov/cibola

Neighborhood: Northeast Heights

PACK "THE PIT"

Albuquerque bursts with school pride for the University of New Mexico Lobos. Cherry-and-silver-clad basketball fans are particularly zealous when they fill every seat in the university's arena, nicknamed "the Pit" because its playing floor lies 37 feet below street level. The Pit has a reputation as being one of the loudest venues in college basketball. It has ranked in the top 25 in attendance for NCAA basketball games for 49 straight years and counting. The cheering crowds pay off for the Lobos, who have won more than 80 percent of their games on their home court. The Pit has also hosted NCAA tournament games. Built in 1966, the Pit was renovated in 2010. No matter who you're cheering for in this arena, remember: Everyone's a Lobo. Woof, woof, woof!

1111 University Blvd. SE, golobos.com

Tickets: (877) 664-8661, unmtickets.com

Neighborhood: University, *Kid Friendly

TRACE THE PAST
AT PETROGLYPH NATIONAL MONUMENT

Native Americans and Spanish residents of the Rio Grande Valley have left indelible cultural influences. They've left physical traces, too—in the black volcanic rocks of Petroglyph National Monument, one of the largest such sites in North America. The monument, on the city's west mesa, protects more than 7,000 acres of land, which is dotted with these 400- to 700-year-old markings. Boca Negra Canyon is the most popular area in the park because it's the monument's only developed area with restrooms, shade structures, and a drinking fountain. The 70-acre section has three self-guided trails offering views of a hundred markings of birds, snakes, spirals, geographic designs, and handprints. For today's Native American peoples and the descendants of Spanish settlers, the land and markings hold deep spiritual significance. Walk softly as you visit.

Intersection of Western Trail and Unser Boulevard Northwest
(505) 899-0205, ext. 335, nps.gov/petr

Neighborhood: Westside, *Kid Friendly

SOAK
AT BETTY'S BATH AND DAY SPA

Betty's Bath and Day Spa is a wellness haven. The spa offers co-ed communal, women-only, and private soaking pools. Adobe walls and shade trees enclose the pools, giving them a faraway feel even though this spa lies within a bustling urban area. Betty's prides itself on having the best massage therapists in town, and it lives up to its promise with deep-tissue, sports, pregnancy, Thai, and sinus-relief options. To make the most of your experience, soak prior to a massage. Betty's also offers a menu of facials and body treatments. Its signature remedy is the Dulce de Cuerpo, a full-body exfoliating treatment that begins with a soothing coconut-oil treatment, followed by hand and foot massages, then the namesake sugar scrub. It's the perfect way to slough off your worries.

1835 Candelaria NW, (505) 341-3456, bettysbath.com

Neighborhood: North Valley

SHRED
AT SANDIA PEAK SKI AREA

Visitors are often surprised Albuquerque gets snow. We do! Even if it's only two inches in the city and it melts by 10 a.m. The mountains receive much more, and Sandia Peak Ski Area is the closest place to take advantage by hitting the slopes. Via the Sandia Peak Tramway, skiers can be making turns within 15 minutes of the western base. Most skiers, however, choose to drive around to the mountain's east side and up to the Double Eagle Day Lodge, where a café, sports shop, and ski school await. The ski area receives an average of 125 inches of snow each year. Thirty runs are accessible via five lifts (three chair lifts and two surface lifts), with more than half of the terrain suiting intermediate skiers. Opening and closing dates depend on snowfall, but the season generally runs from late December through mid-March.

From Albuquerque, take I-40 east to Cedar Crest.
At Exit 175, head north on NM 14 to Sandia Crest Scenic Byway 536.
Follow the byway six miles to the ski area. (505) 242-9052, sandiapeak.com

Neighborhood: East Mountains, *Kid Friendly

TIP
If snowshoeing and cross-country skiing are more your speed, head to the Sandia Crest Trail. For sledding and tubing, opt for the Capulin Snow Play Area.

GLIDE
ALONG THE SANDIA PEAK TRAMWAY

If Albuquerque has an Empire State Building equivalent, this is it. The tram is easily the largest tourist attraction in the city and offers spectacular views of the Duke City and the Rio Grande Valley during the 2.7-mile ride from the foothills to the Sandia Mountains crest. There's another equivalency to the Big Apple attraction here, too: at one point during the trip, the car hangs some 1,000 feet above Big Canyon, at approximately the same height above the ground as the top of the Empire State Building. The tram made its first voyage in 1966. (It has received regular maintenance and safety testing throughout its life.) At the summit, first catch your breath: you're standing at 10,378 feet of elevation. Then, take in the 11,000 square miles of views possible from this vantage point, including those of Mount Taylor, Cabezon peak, and the Jemez Mountains.

30 Tramway Rd. NE, (505) 856-6419, sandiapeak.com

Neighborhood: Northeast Heights, *Kid Friendly

TIP

Make reservations for TEN 3, the fine dining restaurant now perched at Sandia Peak. The menu features from-scratch dishes starring locally sourced ingredients. There isn't a bad seat in the house, with floor-to-ceiling windows providing sweeping city views.

HIKE
FOURTH OF JULY CANYON

This Manzano Mountains canyon has fall foliage that rivals the East Coast (albeit on a much smaller scale). Picturesque year-round, the canyon's true fireworks—the fiery leaves of Bigtooth and Rocky Mountain maples—burst in late September to mid-October, when scarlet drapes the trail. Temperature determines when the leaves change. The warmer the weather, the later the leaves will blush. Golden scrub oak bushes enclose the trail like parentheses adding to the fall color and scenery. Fittingly, this route is quite popular during autumn; the remainder of the year, the trail is relatively untraveled. The full trail is a 6.1-mile out-and-back hike; however, leaf peepers can follow the trail for as long or short as they wish beneath the ruby canopy.

Cibola National Forest, Mountainair Ranger District
(505) 847-2990, fs.usda.gov/cibola

Neighborhood: Manzano, *Kid Friendly

TIP
Keep in mind that the drive from the city takes about an hour.

SOAK
IN JEMEZ SPRINGS

Getting to the village of Jemez Springs, 60 miles northwest of Albuquerque, is half the fun: you'll drive the Jemez Mountain Trail, a National Scenic Byway that traces the Jemez River past red rocks and sheer canyon cliffs into the Jemez Mountains. Once you've arrived in the hamlet, you can dip into healing mineral waters at the Jemez Springs Bath House or Jemez Hot Springs. Giggling Springs's glistening turquoise pools on the river's edge blend the comfort of a resort and the experience of being in the open air. Outdoor adventurers crave the natural hot springs in the Jemez Mountains. There are two popular treks: From the Battleship Rock parking lot, a 3.5-mile hike (round-trip) leads to the McCauley Hot Springs, where warm waters will soothe any time of year. North of Jemez Springs, off NM 4, a short trail leads to the river and up to the smaller Spence Hot Springs, which keeps a constant temperature of 95 degrees.

Sixty miles north of Albuquerque, off NM 4, jemezsprings.org

Neighborhood: Jemez Springs, *Kid Friendly

Jemez Springs Bath House
62 Jemez Springs Plaza, (575) 829-3303, jemezspringsbathhouse.com

Jemez Hot Springs
40 Abousleman Loop, (575) 829-9175, jemezhotsprings.com

ROOT
FOR THE HOME TEAM

Get taken out to the ball game at Isotopes Park, where you can cheer for the Albuquerque Isotopes. The AAA baseball team, minor-league farm team for the Colorado Rockies, debuted in 2003. The team's name has an interesting backstory. An episode of *The Simpsons*, in which Homer protests the Springfield Isotopes' plans to move to Albuquerque by going on a hunger strike, inspired the team's name. The name fits, thanks to Albuquerque's connection to nuclear history. Orbit, the mascot, seems to have experienced some radiation; it's unclear if he's an alien, a dog, a bear, or all three. Regardless, he's quite friendly and helps to make games fun. Check the schedule for games offering fireworks and giveaways. A note about the park dress code: Yes, Isotopes gear is in vogue, but so is Albuquerque Dukes gear. The Dukes were the city's team until 2000, and Burqueños still proudly wear the team's jerseys and hats.

1601 Avenida Cesar Chavez SE, (505) 222-4058, abqisotopes.com

Neighborhood: University, *Kid Friendly

TIP
If you want to participate in any of the between-inning on-field games, sign up at the guest services booth when you enter the park.

HIKE
KASHA-KATUWE TENT ROCKS NATIONAL MONUMENT

The distinct volcanic formations here can be seen in only a handful of other places in the world, including Cappadocia, Turkey. The Duke City is lucky to have them in its backyard within an hour's drive. *Kasha-Katuwe* means "white cliffs" in the traditional Keresan language of nearby Cochiti Pueblo, but alabaster is just one earthen hue you'll see at this national monument. The easy 1.2-mile Cave Loop Trail wanders among red-rock mesas; the 1.5-mile Canyon Trail treks through a slot canyon. A bit of scrambling and a few switchbacks lead to a mesa top offering views of the pinnacles, some of which tower 90 feet. Ancient volcanos cast ash over this landscape. Wind and rain later carved the pumice into these unique formations. In the arroyos, you may spot translucent obsidian (volcanic glass) orbs, another testament to the monument's geological past.

55 miles north of Albuquerque, off Indian Service Route 92
(505) 761-8700, blm.gov/visit/kktr

Neighborhood: Cochiti, *Kid Friendly

WATCH THE SUNSET
AT VOLCANOES DAY USE AREA

When the sun sets over Albuquerque, it's difficult to decide where to look: to the multi-hued west, where the sun dips below the horizon, or to the east, to see the Sandia Mountains in alpenglow. Light glinting off the potassium feldspar in the granite mountains give the hills their distinctive watermelon hue. (*Sandia* means "watermelon" in Spanish, though the mountains' name comes from the nearby Sandia Pueblo, not the fruit.) One of the best places to watch the sunset is from the Volcanoes Day Use Area, part of Petroglyph National Monument. There, you can hike loop trails up the three sister volcanoes that dot the western mesa (JA, Black, and Vulcan), each offering spectacular city and mountain views—especially at sunset.

Off Atrisco Vista Boulevard, (505) 899-0205, nps.gov/petr

Neighborhood: Westside, *Kid Friendly

TIP

If you plan to watch the sunset from the Volcanoes Day Use Area, be sure to leave your car outside the park gates. The parking lot is closed—and the gate locked—promptly at 5 p.m.

TAKE AN
OTHERWORLDLY WALK
AT OJITO WILDERNESS AREA

One of two wilderness areas in Albuquerque's immediate orbit, Ojito, is the harder to love. Badlands, steep mesas, and box canyons make up the landscape here—quite austere compared to the forested surroundings of Sandia Mountain Wilderness. However, the bands of rust, ochre, and chalk shale make this more than 11,000-acre landscape of badlands imminently tantalizing, which is likely why they were protected in 2005 for their pristine beauty. There are two trails for trekking here. The Seismosaurus Trail travels through arroyos and across mesa tops. The trail is named for the fossil that hikers stumbled upon here; it's one of many that's been unearthed in the fossil-rich Jurassic-era Morrison Formation sandstone. The Hoodoo Trail, named for its signature formations, wends among marbled pinnacles. The area is also open to primitive camping.

60 miles northwest of Albuquerque, off US 550, (505) 761-8700, blm.gov

Neighborhood: Outside of Bernalillo, *Kid Friendly

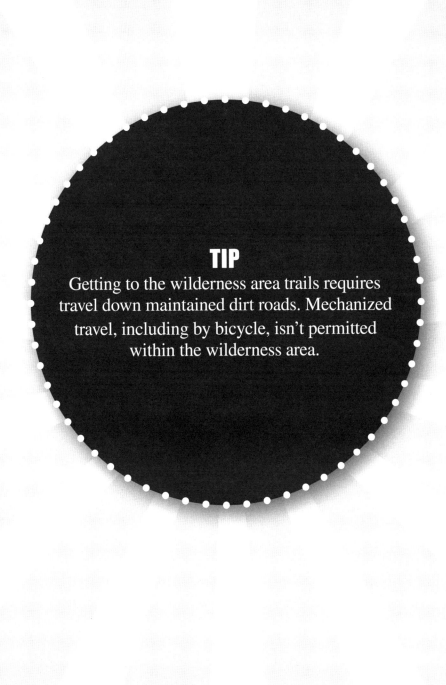

TIP

Getting to the wilderness area trails requires travel down maintained dirt roads. Mechanized travel, including by bicycle, isn't permitted within the wilderness area.

Dancer at Indian Pueblo
Cultural Center

CULTURE AND HISTORY

CELEBRATE CULTURE
AT THE GATHERING
OF NATIONS POW WOW

During the grand entry to this competitive pow wow each April, a drumbeat announces the presence of 3,000 Native people streaming into Tingley Coliseum at Expo New Mexico. The singers' voices rise above even the jingling, pounding footsteps of the dancers who swirl in colorful regalia. Participants, who hail from some 500 tribes in the US, Canada, and Mexico, preserve their traditional cultures and share them with 15,000 attendees through dances like jingle, fancy, grass, and eagle. The largest pow wow in the US also includes the Miss Indian World pageant, a horse-and-rider regalia parade, and an Indian Traders Market, where you'll find everything from cone jingles for fancy-dance dresses to Navajo jewelry. Traditional and contemporary Native musicians play at Stage 49, with groups ranging from rock to hip-hop.

(505) 836-2810, gatheringofnations.com

Neighborhood: Midtown, *Kid Friendly

SHOUT ¡OLÉ!
AT TABLAO FLAMENCO ALBUQUERQUE

Albuquerque's distinctive flamenco scene is an inheritance of its Spanish culture. The National Institute of Flamenco has preserved the dance and music's artistry for decades with classes, performances, and festivals. The art now has a year-round venue with Tablao Flamenco Albuquerque, a dedicated space within Hotel Albuquerque. The intimate space presents performances several times a week as flamenco was meant to be seen—with guests gathered around tables sipping sangria, munching on tapas, and enjoying performances just steps away. The cante flamenco (song) and toque (playing of the guitar) reverberate around a couple dozen tables as the dancers articulate every emotional nuance of this passionate art with twirls of their hands, swishes of fringed skirts, and stomps of their feet.

Hotel Albuquerque
800 Rio Grande Blvd. NW, (505) 222-8797, tablaoflamenco.org

Neighborhood: Old Town

TIP

The National Institute of Flamenco hosts the Festival Flamenco Alburquerque each June. Regarded as the longest-standing flamenco event outside Spain, the weeklong event draws talents from around the globe for public performances and master classes. nationalinstituteofflamenco.org

---

SPARKLE
AT THE TWINKLE LIGHT PARADE

This family-friendly holiday celebration dazzles along Central Avenue each December. Although applications are required to participate, nearly any community group can join the festivities with a lighted float or group decked out in glowing gear. The groups who organize floats have included the City of Albuquerque's Solid Waste Management Division, private businesses, car clubs, and individual families. The only real requirement is that their floats or presentations (like marching Girl Scouts) must dazzle with holiday spirit, and they certainly do. Local celebrities turn out to judge the floats. The parade travels a mile through Nob Hill from Washington Street NE west to Girard Boulevard NE. Just like in the Macy's Thanksgiving Day Parade, St. Nick ends the parade and ushers in the holiday season in the Duke City.

cabq.gov/artsculture

Neighborhood: Nob Hill, *Kid Friendly

VIEW THE MURALS
AT CORONADO HISTORIC SITE

This monument is named for Francisco Vasquez de Coronado, whose entrada camped near Kuaua Pueblo (meaning "evergreen" in the Tiwa language) between 1540 and 1542 during its search for the fabled Seven Cities of Gold. When Museum of New Mexico archaeologists excavated the pueblo in the 1930s they discovered a noteworthy kiva (ceremonial chamber). The ceremonial chamber is square (most are round). It also contained many layers of murals that are some of the finest examples of pre-Columbian art found in the US; the murals were painted as frescoes in the 15th century. You can see 14 sections of the original murals in the visitor center. With a guide or ranger escort, you can visit the square kiva where Ma Pe Wi, a Zia Pueblo artist, recreated the murals in 1938. They were restored in 2013. The frescoes depict soaring eagles and swallows, seeds, and life-giving raindrops.

485 Kuaua Rd., (505) 867-5351, nmhistoricsites.org/coronado

Neighborhood: Bernalillo, *Kid Friendly

BROWSE
THE NATIONAL HISPANIC CULTURAL CENTER

This world-class center is one of a kind in the US. It's the only center to celebrate Hispanic and all Latin American cultures under one umbrella. The sprawling campus includes a visual arts museum, several performance halls, an education building, and a genealogy center. The visual arts collection is a standout: The 11,000-square-foot gallery space exhibits exciting contemporary and traditional works from renowned Latin American, Spanish, and Nuevo Mexicano artists such as Charles M. Carrillo and Luis Jimenez, as well as changing exhibits. It hosts some 700 events a year—from film screenings to world-class music concerts and art openings—so it's a rare night you'll find the center's calendar blank. No wonder it's become one of the top-attended cultural institutions in the state.

1701 4th St. SW, (505) 246-2261, nhccnm.org

Neighborhood: Barelas, *Kid Friendly (depending on the show)

TIP

Don't miss the Torreón (watchtower) at the entrance. Inside, *Mundos de Mestizaje* retells 3,000 years of Hispanic history and has earned acclaim as the largest concave fresco in North America. The true fresco by Santa Fe artist Frederico Vigil took more than 10 years to design and paint; Vigil used local models for his depictions of Toltecs, Mayans, medieval Spanish, and early Albuquerqueans, all of whom figure in the mural.

SIT BACK
FOR FIRST FRIDAY FRACTALS

Your inner nerd can have a night out on the town at First Friday Fractals, a monthly show during which fractals swirl across the full dome of the planetarium at the New Mexico Museum of Natural History and Science. Fractals, both a natural and mathematical phenomenon, are repeating patterns that display at every scale, and these designs come to life in the domed presentation. The first of two different show, *First Friday Fractals*, features original music and narration. A member of the Fractal Foundation, a nonprofit educational organization and creators of the show, describes the phenomenon as the multicolored visualizations swirl and dazzle. Later in the evening, the second show, *Fractals Rock!*, offers a similar immersive journey with less explanation. Both are visually stunning.

New Mexico Museum of Natural History and Science
1801 Mountain Rd. NW, (505) 841-2800, nmnaturalhistory.org

Neighborhood: Old Town, *Kid Friendly

TIP

Buy your tickets in advance, as these shows typically sell out. Online ticket sales end at noon on the day of the show.

GALLERY HOP
AT ALBUQUERQUE ARTWALK

An independent arts organization and community event, Albuquerque Artwalk organizes monthly exhibitions and art markets downtown and in Barelas. During these first Friday happenings, the neighborhoods thrum with outdoor artist performances, vendor booths lining Central Avenue, and food trucks. Participating galleries, restaurants, breweries, and coffee houses debut shows, so this is a promising opportunity to peruse the latest work from the city's top established artists as well as emerging talents. Head to the organization's website for a map of the latest events and openings. The maps also highlight an artist of the month. The event is held in conjunction with the Albuquerque ARTScrawl, a city-wide, self-guided event that the Albuquerque Art Business Association created in 2005.

abqartwalk.com

Neighborhoods: Downtown and Barelas
*Kid Friendly (depending on the show)

FLY HIGH
AT THE ALBUQUERQUE
INTERNATIONAL BALLOON FIESTA

The Albuquerque International Balloon Fiesta is the city's largest sporting event and its most popular festival rolled into one. The festival debuted with 13 hot-air balloons in a mall parking lot in 1972. From its humble beginnings, it has become the largest hot-air balloon gathering in the world. Usually, more than 500 hot-air balloon teams attend the event. The nine-day fiesta, which is held annually the first week of October, features a variety of events. During the popular morning mass ascensions attendees watch the balloons inflate and take off in waves from Balloon Fiesta Park. For a couple hours, the balloons ride the drafts of the "Albuquerque box"—a weather phenomenon that keeps the balloonists aloft over the city for long flights and has helped establish the city's reputation as a flying destination.

5000 Balloon Fiesta Pkwy. NE, (888) 422-7277 or (505) 821-1000
balloonfiesta.com

Neighborhood: Northeast Heights, *Kid Friendly

TIPS

Although there's parking available at Balloon Fiesta Park, the best way to arrive is via the park-and-ride shuttle buses from satellite locations around the city. Or even better, come by bike; you can check your wheels at the bicycle valet.

There are always balloons over Burque. The Anderson Abruzzo Albuquerque International Balloon Museum is open year-round and tells the history of the sport both around the globe and in town. The most enthralling artifacts are the original and replica versions of historic crafts, including the *Double Eagle II*, in which Albuquerque balloonists Maxie Anderson and Ben Abruzzo, along with Larry Newman, completed the first manned crossing of the Atlantic Ocean in 1978, and the balloon used by Troy Bradley (a local) and Leonid Tiukhtyaev when they set the world records for distance and flight duration in 2015.

9201 Balloon Museum Dr. NE, (505) 768-6020, balloonmuseum.com

SPEND AN EVENING
WITH THE BARD

Grab a (free!) seat during the month-long run of the New Mexico Shakespeare Festival, held on select dates each summer. At last count, it was one of only 14 free Shakespeare festivals in the US and only one of two west of the Mississippi. The Vortex Theatre founded a Shakespeare program, originally called "Will Power," in 2010. After hosting the festival at Albuquerque's Civic Plaza for several years, the celebration of the Bard moved to New Mexico Veterans Memorial Park in 2019. Previous seasons have included iconic works such as *Romeo and Juliet* and *Hamlet*. There's something special about seeing one of the Bard's productions in the open air, as they were originally performed. And the experience is even more special with the Sandia Mountains at sunset as the backdrop.

Veterans Memorial Park at New Mexico Veterans Memorial
1100 Louisiana Blvd. SE, newmexicoshakespearefest.org

Neighborhood: Southeast Heights, *Kid Friendly (depending on the play)

TAKE
A PUBLIC ART WALK

Albuquerque boasts one of the oldest public art programs in the country. In 1978, voters passed the Art in Municipal Places Ordinance, which has since funded over 1,000 works. Pieces can be found all over the city, from the Albuquerque International Sunport to the Westside. There are more than 400 sculptures, murals, paintings, and mosaics in downtown alone, and the Albuquerque Convention Center has a large collection of pieces within the building and easily visible to visitors. A mosaic dances on the building's exterior. Students from the Mayor's Art Summer Institute at Harwood Art Center created it and have added to it each summer over the course of more than a decade; it tells the story of New Mexico's cultural history. Find suggested tours and information about the individual works on the City of Albuquerque's Public Art website.

cabq.gov

Neighborhood: Citywide, *Kid Friendly

TIP
The "Chevy on a Stick" (created by Barbara Grygutis and officially known as *Cruising San Mateo I* before it earned its nickname in the early 1990s) is one of the city's most notable—and most controversial—public art pieces. The sculpture, in which a full-sized, tiled car sits atop an arch, has become a must-do photo op.

WATCH A DANCE
AT THE INDIAN PUEBLO
CULTURAL CENTER

In New Mexico, traditional Native American dances, which have deep cultural roots in each pueblo and tribe, are reflections of yesteryear and today. Usually, seeing such dances requires a road trip. In town, the Indian Pueblo Cultural Center hosts groups from different pueblos and tribes to share this facet of their cultures most weekends and more often during peak times, such as during the Albuquerque International Balloon Fiesta. You may encounter the Olla Maidens from Zuni Pueblo, the Red Turtle Dancers from Pojoaque Pueblo, or buffalo dancers from Jemez Pueblo. The Indian Pueblo Cultural Center is unique in the world because it is collectively owned by the state's 19 pueblos. The center is the preeminent place to learn about the pueblos' history, culture, and art. Beyond the dances, the museum presents a permanent exhibit, *We Are of This Place*, that tells the story of the Pueblo people from their perspective.

2401 12th St. NW, (505) 843-7270, indianpueblo.org

Neighborhood: North Valley, *Kid Friendly

SEE AN INDIE FLICK
AT THE GUILD CINEMA

The Guild is Albuquerque's independent film house. The single-screen theater shows low-budget, foreign, and off-the-radar films, from classic cult hits to newly produced film festival darlings. Oscar-nominated shorts (animated, documentary, and live action) and full-length documentaries get their day on the big screen here during awards season. The Guild Art Theatre debuted on February 16, 1966, as an adult theater. It's had a rocky run with various closures and rebirths, and it's had identities from an adult movie venue to a revival theater house. After starting as a projectionist in 1997, owner Keif Henley bought it in 2004 and has kept it alive, even throughout the pandemic. It's the only independent art house theater still operating in the sea of the Duke City's multiplexes.

3405 Central Ave. NE, (505) 255-1848, guildcinema.com

Neighborhood: Nob Hill

TIP
The intimate house has only a few dozen seats, so arrive early to find one and get your popcorn. Don't miss the red-chile-powder topping.

RUN AWAY
TO THE OT CIRCUS

Everyone belongs at the OT Circus. Founded by occupational therapist Victoria Van Dame in 2013, the nonprofit organization uses creativity and various therapeutic methods to bring artists together. The artists range from emerging and experienced, and many face physical or emotional challenges. "We need to cultivate and help people who wouldn't otherwise think their art is any good, or acceptable. Just because you have depression, you're on hospice, or you have a physical disability doesn't mean you can't have a show," she says. During the pandemic, the OT Circus took its usually in-person shows online by creating a diverse digital art market. But don't miss the opportunity to see the works in person (often during Albuquerque Artwalk) if you can. Meeting the artists makes the experience all the richer.

709 Central Ave. NW, (505) 249-2231, otcircus.com

Neighborhood: Downtown, *Kid Friendly (depending on the exhibition)

EARN A CERTIFICATE OF BRAVERY
AT THE AMERICAN INTERNATIONAL RATTLESNAKE MUSEUM

To earn your certificate of bravery here, you'll have to navigate three rooms packed with terrariums of often-feared creatures. It's billed as the largest live collection of different species of rattlesnakes in the world—greater even than those at the San Diego, National, and Denver Zoos. The displays include species such as the eastern diamondback, one of the most dangerous snakes in the world; a banded rock rattlesnake; and a red diamond rattlesnake. Rattlesnakes aren't the only residents here. It also includes other snakes such as boas, bull snakes, and pythons, and reptiles such as lizards, box turtles, and desert tortoises. Always the goal is to educate and inform—and the more you know about these graceful creatures, the less intimidating they become for many visitors.

202 San Felipe St. NW, (505) 242-6569, rattlesnakes.com

Neighborhood: Old Town, *Kid Friendly

TOUR
BREAKING BAD FILMING LOCATIONS

Breaking Bad, the TV drama that put Albuquerque on the pop-culture map, had locals asking if the show about a teacher turned meth cook made the city look tough—or just tragic. Either way, the show, which was both filmed and set in the Duke City, continues to attract fans to visit the real-life locations that appeared on the AMC drama—even more than 10 years after the show's finale. For a self-guided tour, see the following list. For a guided one, hitch a ride on a *Breaking Bad* RV Tour. Guides lead the tours on one of the three 1986 Fleetwood Bounder RVs that appeared on the show. It visits 17 filming locations, including Tuco's office (on the second floor of real-life Java Joe's) and Combo's corner (at Second Street and Hazeldine Avenue). The prequel, *Better Call Saul*, aired from 2015 to 2022—and added even more locales for completists to visit.

breakingbadrvtours.com, Neighborhood: Citywide

MUST-SEE *BREAKING BAD* FILMING LOCATIONS

Crossroads Motel
1001 Central Ave. NE

Dog House Drive In
1216 Central Ave. NW

Jesse Pinkman's House*
Northeast corner of
Los Alamos Avenue and
16th Street Southwest

**Mister Car Wash, a.k.a.
A1A Car Wash**
9516 Snow Heights Cir. NE

John B. Robert Dam
Juan Tabo Boulevard
Northeast between
Montgomery Boulevard
and Spain Road

Walter White's House*
3828 Piermont Dr. NE
(Intersection of Piermont
Drive and Orlando Place)

**Twisters, a.k.a.
Los Pollos Hermanos**
4257 Isleta Blvd. SW

MUST-SEE *BETTER CALL SAUL* FILMING LOCATIONS

Chuck's House*
1607 San Cristobal Rd. SW

Mike's House*
204 Edith Blvd. NE

Day Spa and Nail, a.k.a. Jimmy's Office
160 Juan Tabo Blvd. NE

*Please note: These are private residences. Stay on the sidewalk and be respectful of the owners' wishes and privacy. The owners of the real-life Walter White house even erected a fence around the property to keep fans at bay. Hey, you probably would, too, after regularly having pizzas thrown on your roof.

BROWSE
THE SOUTH BROADWAY CULTURAL CENTER

Perhaps because of its off-the-beaten path location this art gem often escapes notice. However, its eight-times-a-year exhibitions are well worth a visit. The customary Día de los Muertos exhibition is a perennial favorite. People of Mexican heritage in and outside that country celebrate the Day of the Dead, which honors the lives of loved ones who have passed. During the annual cultural center exhibition, artists construct ofrendas (shrines/offerings) that pay homage to relatives, pop icons, and historical figures alike with photos, mementos, offerings, flowers, and candles. The center also houses the John Lewis Theatre (named after the jazz pianist and longtime Albuquerquean), which hosts artist talks, literary events, and other events. The city-owned theater lies in one of Albuquerque's oldest neighborhoods, so it's also a fitting jumping off point for further explorations in the area.

1025 Broadway Blvd. SE, (505) 848-1320
cabq.gov/artsculture/south-broadway-cultural-center

Neighborhood: South Broadway

SEE AN EXHIBITION
AT HARWOOD ART CENTER

As one of the most vibrant destinations in the city, there's always something happening at the Harwood. It's a lifelong-learning center and an outreach program of Escuela del Sol Montessori, which, along with the school and art spaces, covers a full city block downtown. The Harwood supports selected emerging artists through a professional development program and hosts a couple floors of art studios. Once a year, the artists open the doors so the public can see their workspaces and view works in progress. For the finished results, check out the Harwood's downstairs gallery space, which mounts a handful of curated shows each year. Bitten by the art bug? The Harwood hosts adult art workshops in everything from journaling to silversmithing.

1114 7th St. NW, (505) 242-6367, harwoodartcenter.org

Neighborhood: Downtown

TIP

The Harwood's annual *12x12 Fundraising Exhibition* features works by established, emerging, and youth artists. The works are sold for a flat rate and the artist is only revealed once sold. It's a chance to support a nonprofit—and potentially to get a work from a phenomenal artist at a bargain price.

EXPLORE
THE UNIVERSITY OF NEW MEXICO ART MUSEUM

Unless you're a university student, this museum may be off your radar. The quality exhibitions here should place the museum squarely on it. Founded in 1962, the art museum possesses a 30,000-piece permanent collection making it the largest free-to-view art collection in the state. The collection includes notable works of photography thanks to the vision of the first director Van Deren Coke, who made it one of the first universities in the country to begin collecting these images. It also houses the 2,400-strong Raymond Jonson collection from the founder of the Transcendental Painting Group and many of his contemporaries, including Agnes Martin, Elaine DeKooning, Richard Diebenkorn, and Josef Albers. Finally, it also maintains the archives of the Tamarind Institute (see that entry in this guide for more information). The museum also hangs a changing series of shows in photography, sculpture, painting, as well as significant installations.

Redondo Drive and Stanford Drive (at the University of New Mexico Center for the Arts), (505) 277-4001, artmuseum.unm.edu

Neighborhood: University

TIP

While you're on campus, check out
the Maxwell Museum of Anthropology,
where two permanent exhibits explore the
ancient history of Southwest peoples.
1 University Blvd. NE, (505) 277-4405
unm.edu/~maxwell

TIME TRAVEL
AT ALBUQUERQUE MUSEUM

With its *Only in Albuquerque* history exhibition, this gem is a repository of the city's past. The exhibit tells the story of the Rio Grande Valley through displays showing Navajo and Pueblo blankets that double as historical artifacts and art, farm and ranch tools, and early European maps of New Spain. The museum's collection of helmets, swords, and colonial European armor is considered among the best in the US. On Albuquerque's fertile creative grounds, history is woven with art. The creatives featured in the museum's permanent art exhibit, *Common Ground: Art in New Mexico*, reads like a who's-who list of Southwest art: it includes the works of Ernest L. Blumenschein, Georgia O'Keeffe, and Fritz Scholder, to name a few. Check the schedule for national and international traveling exhibitions.

2000 Mountain Rd. NW, (505) 243-7255, albuquerquemuseum.org

Neighborhood: Old Town, *Kid Friendly

TIPS

The museum offers free admission several times each month: every Sunday from 9 a.m. to 1 p.m.; the first Wednesday of the month from 9 a.m. to 5 p.m.; and the third Thursday of the month from 5 to 8 p.m. Third Thursday programs feature special programming with live music, exhibition talks, art projects, yoga classes, and more.

If bitten by the history bug, head to Casa San Ysidro: The Gutiérrez/Minge House in Corrales, a satellite of the Albuquerque Museum, to see New Mexican art and furnishings displayed in an adobe home. cabq.gov/artsculture/albuquerque-museum/ casa-san-ysidro

FEEL THE GLOW
WITH LUMINARIAS IN OLD TOWN

Duke City denizens' favorite holiday tradition is seeing luminarias on Christmas Eve. These decorations may be modest (a paper bag weighted down with sand and a small candle lit inside), but the ethereal flickering of thousands makes the holiday merry and bright. The best neighborhoods to see them are Old Town and the Country Club, where businesses and residences line adobe walls and walkways with the lanterns. For the holiday, the City of Albuquerque turns its public buses into tour coaches to drive passengers through these renowned neighborhoods to see the lights while staying warm. If you want to walk rather than ride, visit Old Town after 9 p.m. (my favorite time), when the crowds, cars, and buses have dissipated.

Neighborhoods: Old Town and Country Club, *Kid Friendly

TIP

Tickets for the bus tours sell out early—sometimes in one day. To ensure you get one, buy yours the day after Thanksgiving, when tickets go on sale. cabq.gov

DICTION DEBATE

Albuquerqueans refer to the bagged beauties as *luminarias*. However, in northern New Mexico, a paper bag with a candle inside is called a *farolito* and small bonfires *luminarias*. Who's right? Whomever you're speaking to at the time.

CRUISE ROUTE 66

Follow the neon along 18 miles of old Route 66 through Albuquerque. The historic Mother Road, now Central Avenue, bisects the city on its path from Chicago to Los Angeles. Following its route through the Duke City, you'll pass some of the city's most popular neighborhoods and attractions, including Nob Hill, a trendy shopping area; the University of New Mexico; downtown and Old Town; the ABQ BioPark Aquarium and Botanic Garden; and the volcanoes that hug the city's western edge. Take note of the intersection of Central Avenue and Fourth Street: Fourth Street was part of the original route (1926–1937) that ran north/south through Albuquerque along this existing road. In 1931, the route was realigned along an east/west trajectory. This is one of the few places that the two phases of the road intersect at a 90-degree angle.

rt66nm.org

Neighborhood: Citywide, *Kid Friendly

RIDE
A STUCCO TROLLEY

At ABQ Trolley Co., you'll tour the city in a one-of-a-kind ride: a stucco-covered trolley. Two Albuquerque tourism professionals, Jesse Herron and Mike Silva, dreamed up the trolley tour company and launched it in 2009. The two had big dreams and now oversee the Albuquerque Tourism & Sightseeing Factory, which has branched out to pedal tours, ghost walks, and digital scavenger hunts. But its flagship is still its unique vehicle and the Best of ABQ City Tour. The narrated tour includes Duke City landmarks, as well as lesser-known attractions and local trivia that will have even long-term residents quizzing themselves. If you don't want to hop on board with the headlining tour, seasonal and themed outings have trekked to the Albuquerque International Balloon Fiesta, toured holiday lights, and visited *Breaking Bad* filming locations.

Inside Hotel Albuquerque
800 Rio Grande Blvd. NW, (505) 200-2642, tourabq.com/abqtrolley

Neighborhood: Old Town, *Kid Friendly

DANCE
OVER TO KESHET CENTER FOR THE ARTS

Shira Greenberg founded Keshet Dance Company in 1996 as a professional repertory to bring contemporary dance to the Duke City. Since then, Keshet has grown into a multifaceted arts organization. It remains notable for its professional contemporary dance performances, as well as for its community-driven performances with dancers of many varieties, including those who use mobility devices and people with all levels of physical and developmental abilities. The 30,000-square-foot Center for the Arts—and attached Ideas and Innovation Center—may be hidden in a warehouse district, but its studios, black-box spaces, and performance venues have become draws thanks to visiting choreographers and dance groups from across the globe, resident theater troupes, and even adult and children's dance classes.

4121 Cutler Ave. NE, (505) 224-9808, keshetarts.org

Neighborhood: Midtown, *Kid Friendly

TIP
Take note of the mural on Keshet Center for the Arts' exterior. Painted in 2018, *Momentous Momentum Moments* by Mick Burson is the largest in the state. It took 91 gallons of paint to complete and covers 13,400 square feet.

GO TRUE BLUE
AT THE TURQUOISE MUSEUM

This privately owned museum explores all aspects of the color and stone that enraptures the Southwest. Members of the Lowry family, including the youngest, fifth-generation, oversee the museum and are sometimes on hand during tours. The museum's stately location befits the collection. It's housed in the Gertrude Zachary Castle, so named for the late jewelry designer who created and owned the home turned museum. The museum entrance sets the stage with a 94-string, three-story glittering turquoise chandelier. The museum's first room is also a showstopper with world-class pieces, such as the George Washington Stone, a chunk of turquoise cut into the shape of the founder's face on happy accident. Subsequent rooms highlight gems from around the world; teach the mining and lapidary process; and explain the difference between natural, imitation, and various forms of stabilized turquoise. These pieces represent a portion of J. C. Zachary Jr.'s (a.k.a. "the King of Turquoise") collection.

400 2nd St. SW, (505) 433-3684, turquoisemuseum.com

Neighborhood: Downtown

GET HANDS ON
AT ¡EXPLORA!

At this experiential-learning center, visitors learn by doing. They have so much fun, they hardly know they're doing so. Some 250 science, technology, engineering, art, and math exhibits stretch over two floors with displays devoted to gravity, water, light, shadow, color, and chain reactions. Art-loving kiddos can watch their sketches come to life as digital projections and play in the crafts workshop. In spring 2022, the learning center was still undergoing construction for a $4 million expansion. Dubbed X-Studio, the addition will focus on teens interested in training for jobs in STEAM with exhibits on robotry, 3-D printers, and more. By day, the science center is aimed at kids, but sometimes the center opens for adults-only evenings when the post-18 set can play in the bubbles without worrying about elbowing a toddler in an overly enthusiastic moment.

1701 Mountain Rd. NW, (505) 224-8300, explora.us

Neighborhood: Old Town, *Kid Friendly

GLOW
AT THE RIVER OF LIGHTS

In its more than 25-year history, the River of Lights has become one of Albuquerque's favorite holiday traditions. It began in 1997 as a fundraiser for the ABQ BioPark, and it continues to bring in vital funds for important projects across the zoo, aquarium, and botanical garden. The display glitters with millions of lights and nearly 600 displays stretching across the grounds of the ABQ BioPark Botanic Garden from Thanksgiving weekend through the end of December. The light display grows every year. Previous fan favorites have included the T-rex, Pegasus, flowers larger than humans, penguins, and a cow being beamed into a UFO. It ranks as the state's largest walk-through light show and earned a spot as one of the top 10 holiday light displays in the US in 2021.

2601 Central Ave. NW, (505) 764-6200
cabq.gov/artsculture/biopark/events/river-of-lights

Neighborhood: West Downtown, *Kid Friendly

TIP

Parking at the ABQ BioPark Botanic Garden is limited. Additional parking is available at the zoo; a park-and-ride bus delivers you to the garden grounds.

PERUSE 516 ARTS

This non-collecting contemporary art museum displays some of the most intriguing and provocative visual art in the city. The organization presents local, national, and international artists alike. It has particularly enhanced regional artists as a partner of the Andy Warhol Foundation for the Visual Arts. No matter where they're from, risk taking and experimentation are hallmarks among artists the curatorial team selects to exhibit here. The two-story, light-filled gallery setting suits the high-end installations and multimedia creations frequently displayed here. In addition, 516 ARTS usually hosts a lively schedule of gallery talks, artist panels, workshops, and trunk shows. The organization has also made its mark on downtown's appearance with a series of murals on and near Central Avenue; duck inside the gallery to pick up a walking-tour map.

516 Central Ave. SW, (505) 242-1445, 516arts.org

Neighborhood: Downtown

DRIVE
EL CAMINO REAL

Traveling the "royal road" or "king's highway" is a trip through 400 years of Southwest heritage. El Camino Real de Tierra Adentro traveled a route nearly as long as its formal name. It spanned 1,600 miles from Mexico City through what became the state of New Mexico. Juan de Oñate's 1598 expedition defined the trail's route and length. After this expedition, the route became a commerce artery and the earliest Euro-American trade route in the US. However, it brought as many people into today's New Mexico as it did goods. Settlers, priests, traders, enslaved people, and prisoners of war all followed this route. Today, you can drive sections of this historic route, including along NM 313 (a.k.a. "Camino del Pueblo and El Camino Real") through the town of Bernalillo. The route turns into Fourth Street in Albuquerque and extends to the south.

nps.gov/elca

Neighborhood: Albuquerque/Bernalillo

WALK ON THE WILD SIDE
AT ABQ BIOPARK

A quartet of destinations fall under the umbrella of ABQ BioPark: the Zoo, the Aquarium, the Botanic Garden, and Tingley Beach. The 64-acre Zoo exhibits hundreds of species, including several types of penguins, great apes, and hippopotamuses. An aquarium in the desert? Yes, and a good one, too. Exhibits cover habitats from the Rio Grande to the Gulf Coast, and the 285,000-gallon shark tank is a must see. The Botanic Garden is on the same campus as the Aquarium and features elegant ceremonial gardens, a Mediterranean conservatory, and a Rio Grande farm exhibit. Don't miss the *curandera* garden, which pays homage to traditional healers with herbs and botanicals. Tingley Beach is the closest Albuquerqueans get to beachfront property, with a handful of fishing and recreational lakes set along the Río Grande.

TIP
An electric tram is in the works to connect the ABQ BioPark destinations.

Zoo
903 10th St. SW,

Aquarium and Botanic Garden
2601 Central Ave. NW

Tingley Beach
1800 Tingley Dr. SW
(505) 764-6200, cabq.gov

Neighborhood: Downtown, West Downtown
*Kid Friendly

LET WHIMSY TAKE OVER
AT TINKERTOWN MUSEUM

This is one of the most wonderfully wacky museums you'll ever encounter. Museum founder Ross Ward took more than 40 years to carve and collect the mostly miniature wood-carved figures seen here. Some 1,500 figurines are set in scenes, including a mining town and a circus, Press buttons to see the vignettes come to life. The creations traveled the country during the 1960s and '70s appearing at county fairs and carnivals. However, they found a permanent home in Albuquerque's east mountains when Ward constructed a suitably quirky building to match his collection. The design incorporates some 50,000 glass bottles, as well as wagon wheels and horseshoes. The museum is also chock-a-block with other collections such as wedding cakes couples, bullet pens, and antique tools.

121 Sandia Crest Rd., (505) 281-5233, tinkertown.com

Neighborhood: Outside Albuquerque, Sandia Park

TIP

The museum is open April through October. Have quarters on hand—or get them when you buy your ticket—so you can play Otto, the one-man band, and learn your future from Esmerelda, the animatronic fortuneteller, á la Tom Hanks in *Big*.

DISCOVER SECRET GALLERY

The secret's out on Secret Gallery. Founder, program manager, and curator Gabriel Gallegos originally envisioned the gallery as one leading pop-up installations. That's how it launched in 2019. However, when the pandemic descended, Gallegos decided to put down more permanent roots. The gallery aims to make art accessible to everyone in the community, which it took strides toward by landing in the Barelas neighborhood—not one typically known for the high-end, contemporary Southwest art the gallery exhibits. The gallery currently makes its home in B. Ruppe Drugs, a neighborhood landmark known for its former owner's *curanderismo* (traditional healing methods). Secret Gallery artists don't romanticize the Southwest; rather, they depict its landscapes, people, and culture authentically. And these depictions are even more beautiful—and challenging—for their honesty.

807 4th St. SW, (505) 795-0545, secretgallerysw.com

Neighborhood: Barelas

TIP

Don't miss the show openings here during Albuquerque Artwalk. Can't invest in an original? The gift shop sells prints and other less-expensive works.

MAKE YOUR WAY
TO MADRID

Driving the Turquoise Trail National Scenic Byway, on the east side of the Sandia Mountains, is the perfect day trip from the Duke City. The charming town of Madrid is a pleasant waypoint along the route. On Sundays, local motorcyclists flock in droves to the Mine Shaft Tavern for burgers and live music. The tavern is a throwback to the town's roots, but today there are more artists here than miners. You can spend an afternoon zigzagging across NM 14 to the galleries and eclectic shops that line the scenic route, including mainstays such as Johnsons of Madrid and Indigo Gallery. For a caffeinated pick-me-up—or a night's stay in the bed-and-breakfast—stop at Java Junction. Some of the best bites in town are the Southern-fried selections at the Hollar restaurant.

alabamaantiquetrail.com

TIP

The Madrid Christmas Parade is one of the most eclectic small-town parades you'll ever see. Prepare yourself for vintage cars, bagpipes, and a Christmas yak.

MADRID HOT SPOTS

The Hollar
2849 NM 14, (505) 471-4821
thehollar.com

Java Junction
2855 NM 14, (505) 438-2772
java-junction.com

Johnsons of Madrid
2843 NM 14, (505) 471-1054

Indigo Gallery
2860 NM 14, Ste. D, (505) 438-6202
indigoartgallery.com

Mine Shaft Tavern
2846 NM 14, (505) 473-0743
themineshafttavern.com

BROWSE
THE TAMARIND INSTITUTE

Although it may be below the radar for many Albuquerqueans, the Tamarind Institute has a world-class reputation in the art of lithography. A division of the College of Fine Arts at the University of New Mexico, the institute runs a second-story gallery space that mounts a handful of shows each year as well as artist talks. But this is primarily a working print shop that runs a professional program, sponsoring a couple apprentices a year who earn their master printer certificates. The program also facilitates the work of invited artists who, though celebrated in their respective media, may be creating a lithograph for the first time. Artists who have worked at the institute during its more than 50-year history (it was founded in 1960 in Los Angeles and moved to Albuquerque in 1970) include former associate director Clinton Adams and former technical director Garo Antreasian, Hung Liu, and Jim Dine.

2500 Central Ave. SE, (505) 277-3901, tamarind.unm.edu

Neighborhood: University

TIP

If you want to explore the institute's full archives, the University of New Mexico Art Museum, described elsewhere in this book, keeps an archive of every print created since the institute's founding. The archives can be viewed by appointment.

OBSERVE THE RESCUES
AT WILDLIFE WEST NATURE PARK

Spark, a bobcat, was an illegal pet. Mountain lions True and Zia were orphaned when their mother was shot. Dia, a red-tailed hawk, was shot in the wing and suffers muscle damage. All are now inhabitants of Wildlife West Nature Park. Roger Alink founded the nonprofit park in 1992 with the goal of rescuing native wildlife and educating the public about them. The 122-acre park cares for 23 different species. Enclosures for elk, racoons, mountain lions, foxes, a golden eagle, and other animals dot a 1.25-mile paved trail that winds through juniper trees in Edgewood. None of the animals can be returned to the wild due to injuries or familiarization with humans. "Rather than putting them down, they came to live with us," Alink says. The park offers incredibly close vantages to observe these majestic creatures.

87 N Frontage Rd., Edgewood; (505) 281-7655, wildlifewest.org

Neighborhood: Edgewood, *Kid Friendly

WATCH
THE CORRALES FOURTH OF JULY PARADE

The village of Corrales, just north of Albuquerque, takes its name from the Spanish word for corrals. It lives up to those pastoral beginnings today with sweeping acreage devoted to horses and other domesticated animals. In fact, its charming Independence Day parade places these pets front and center. Anyone is welcome to join the festivities, whether two- or four-legged. Town residents promenade with their dogs, alpacas, donkeys, rabbits, and even chickens—all decked out in red, white, and blue for the occasion, of course. Vintage trucks and bagpipe bands—and the slightly less baritone kazoo band. Bring your own chair and pick a spot along Corrales Road, the main thoroughfare through town that's also lined with charming restaurants, quaint shops, and restaurants. After the parade, join the festivities at La Entrada Park.

corrales-nm.org

Neighborhood: Corrales, *Kid Friendly

TIP

Check Corrales's community calendar for other events throughout the year. The Harvest Festival in October and the Corrales Artist Studio Tour in May also provide prime times to explore this charming community.

CHECK OUT
THE ERNIE PYLE LIBRARY

Pulitzer Prize–winning journalist Ernie Pyle became a household name during World War II thanks to his accounts of soldiers on the frontlines. In 1940, he adopted Albuquerque as his home when he and his wife constructed their 1,145-square-foot house in Nob Hill. An early embedded journalist, Pyle was killed in 1945 by a sniper's bullet on the Japanese island of Ie Shima, but his writings inspired the story of G.I. Joe, which has grown to encompass movies, comic books, and action figures. His quaint five-room home went on to become a branch of the Albuquerque/ Bernalillo County Library system. With books lining every wall, Pyle would likely be proud of his home's transformation. The library memorializes Pyle in historic photographs and a few artifacts, like monogrammed ashtrays, goggles he used through his reporting in the World War II Africa campaign, and a replica of a two-headed lion ring he wore daily on the battlefield.

900 Girard Blvd. SE, (505) 265-2065, abqlibrary.org/erniepyle

Neighborhood: Nob Hill, *Kid Friendly

TAKE A GHOST TOUR
OF OLD TOWN

Whether you're ready to see a specter or just skeptical, this tour is an enjoyable way to learn about the city's past. Guided by ABQ Tours, this walk through Albuquerque's founding neighborhood will take you past the ill-chosen former location of the town graveyard, High Noon Restaurant and Saloon, and down "Scarlett's Alley" to hear chill-inducing stories of murders, hangings, and various misdeeds. You'll hear about sightings, disembodied voices, and stories of objects mysteriously moving. The tales, which include mention of trappers, Confederate soldiers, prostitutes, and blue-collar workers, reflect the many phases of the neighborhood's more than 300-year history— beginning when Albuquerque was just four blocks across and the river still flooded Old Town causing caskets from the San Felipe de Neri cemetery to float around the square.

Plaza Don Luis
303 Romero St. NW, Ste. N120, (505) 246-8687, toursofoldtown.com

Neighborhood: Old Town

TIP
Reservations for the nightly tours are required. ABQ Tours also offers once-a-month late-night moonlight tours. Private tours are also available.

WATCH PALEONTOLOGY IN ACTION
AT THE MUSEUM OF NATURAL HISTORY AND SCIENCE

At the New Mexico Museum of Natural History and Science's *FossilWorks* exhibit, visitors observe volunteers demonstrate the laborious process of extracting fossils from rock. Volunteers complete intensive training before conducting this paleontological work, which can range from a few to hundreds of hours depending on the size and complexity of the specimen. It took thousands of hours of work for volunteers to prepare the partial skeleton of a giant theropod, Saurophaganax, which is now displayed in the museum's Age of the Super Giants Hall. Volunteers also surfaced the skull of Bistahievorsor sealeyi, a.k.a. "the Bisti Beast," a Tyrannosaur species discovered in New Mexico. It's now displayed in the *Cretaceous Seacoast* exhibit. On the whole, the museum guides visitors through time beginning with the Big Bang; through the Cretaceous, when New Mexico was a seascape; and through the age of mammals. If you have kids, don't miss the Naturalist Center, where they can touch specimens and meet native animals.

1801 Mountain Rd. NW, (505) 841-2800, nmnaturalhistory.org

Neighborhood: Old Town, *Kid Friendly

REACT
AT THE NATIONAL MUSEUM
OF NUCLEAR SCIENCE AND HISTORY

This Smithsonian-affiliated institution is the only nationally chartered museum in its field. The museum thoughtfully explores the birth of the Atomic Age, which took place in New Mexico via the Manhattan Project, in Los Alamos, and at the Trinity Site, at White Sands Missile Range, where the first atomic bomb exploded in 1945. Exhibitions consider the bomb's development, which includes notable artifacts such as the flag flying over the Trinity Site on the day of the infamous test; the US's decision to drop the bomb on Japan during World War II; the Cold War; and dawning of the Atomic Age's influence on pop culture. Heritage Park, a nine-acre outdoor exhibit area, features planes, rockets, and a nuclear submarine sail. The museum also explores non-weaponized uses of nuclear energy in its thought-provoking displays.

601 Eubank Blvd. SE, (505) 245-2137, nuclearmuseum.org

Neighborhood: Southeast Heights, *Kid Friendly

SHOPPING AND FASHION

BROWSE OLD TOWN

A trip to this tree-lined plaza is first on many visitors' lists—particularly because it's the city's establishing neighborhood. The city's early dwellers build residences around the now historic square; some buildings there today can trace their origins to the city's 1706 founding or shortly thereafter. Today, merchants have set up shop in these rambling adobes and Territorial buildings. Old Town is a top tourist destination, and there are plenty of trinket shops to prove it. Beyond souvenir basics, there are plenty of galleries and boutiques, too. You may also choose to shop from the Native American craftspeople who lay out blankets with their wares on the plaza. You'll easily spend a few hours wandering down cobblestone pathways and through small courtyards off the plaza. In recent years, more local wine tasting rooms, craft brewery taprooms, and restaurants have popped up to sate your thirst and appetite as you shop.

albuquerqueoldtown.com

Neighborhood: Old Town, *Kid Friendly

OLD TOWN SHOPPING LIST

Albuquerque Photographers' Gallery
This artist co-op includes some of the city's
best artists—and you'll find stunning pictures
of the state's landscapes and people here.
328 San Felipe St. NW, Ste. B, (505) 244-9195
abqphotographersgallery.com

Plaza Don Luis
This shopping plaza features several gift shops,
galleries, and other new additions to the neighborhood.
It also hosts live music, artist talks, and other events
many nights of the week.
303 Romero St., pdlabq.com

Tanner Chaney Galleries
With roots dating to 1875, this shop has
a long history of trading Native American
jewelry, pottery, and rugs. It also offers a
healthy collection of estate and pawn jewelry,
which provides fine opportunities for bargains.
323 Romero St. NW, (505) 247-2242, tannerchaney.com

Treasure House Books & Gifts
This cozy bookshop specializes in titles
by local authors and about the Southwest.
2012 S Plaza St. NW A, (505) 242-7204
treasurehousebooks.net

SHOP
THE RAIL YARDS MARKET

During its May–October season, the Railyard Market is a Sunday staple. Market sellers include local farmers, food purveyors, and artisans who give you the chance to stock up on everything from locally grown chile to a beautiful photograph to hang in your home. The market's location is as notable as are its vendors. The soaring buildings at this site were once part of the largest railroad maintenance shop in the region and, at their height, employed around a quarter of the city's workforce. Light shining through broken panes of clear, green, and blue glass takes on the appearance of industrial stained glass in these monuments to industry. The market is housed in the former blacksmith shop and on the outdoor plaza.

777 1st St. SW, (505) 600-1109, railyardsmarket.org

Neighborhood: Barelas/South Broadway, *Kid Friendly

TIP
Don't miss the holiday market during December.

BROWSE
EL VADO MOTEL

Once a 1937 motor court, El Vado Motel is having a renaissance. In 2017, the motel reopened, but this time not all of its rooms were dedicated to guests. Half of the rooms were turned into intimate restaurants and small shops. Merc 66, one of the most notable shops, is a go-to for Route 66 travelers in search of Mother Road passports, vintage-inspired kitsch, and locally made art and gift items that nod to America's Main Street and other elements of Southwest culture.

El Vado Motel
2500 Central Ave. SW, (505) 361-1667, elvadoabq.com

Merc 66
2500 Central Ave. SW, (505) 238-6469, merc66abq.com

Neighborhood: West Downtown, *Kid Friendly

HOBNOB
IN NOB HILL

Planned by Colonel D. K. B. Sellers, Nob Hill was platted in 1916—just four years after New Mexico became a state. The real-estate developer encouraged residents to move beyond the city's core, in his words "out of the low zone into the ozone," since the neighborhood was then on the city's outskirts. At Carlisle Boulevard, Sellers spied a steep slope that struck him as similar to that of San Francisco's Nob Hill and decided to adopt that more famous district's name. A hundred years on, the neighborhood still feels young at heart, with more than 250 independent shops, restaurants, galleries, and bars unfolding from Central Avenue. It's one of the city's top shopping areas for local goods. The best part: everything's within walking distance. So, park the car and enjoy.

nobhillmainstreet.org

Neighborhood: Nob Hill

NOB HILL SHOPPING LIST

IMEC
Jewelry is wearable art, particularly here at the
International Metalsmithing Exhibition Center.
101 Amherst Dr. SE, (505) 265-8352, shopimec.com

Mariposa Gallery
This contemporary crafts gallery curates a
collection that lives up to its tag line: curiouser
and curiouser. Pulling from its stable of eclectic
represented artists, the gallery presents monthly
exhibits based on a theme or a single artist's works.
3500 Central Ave. SE, (505) 268-6828
mariposa-gallery.com

New Mexico United Shop
The New Mexico United team store bleeds black and yellow.
3500 Central Ave. SE, (505) 209-7529
shop.newmexicoutd.com

Ooh! Aah! Jewelry
A neighborhood staple since 1988, the
shop sells unique and stylish jewelry.
110 Amherst Dr. SE, (505) 265-7170, oohaahjewelry.com

Organic Books
Browse used books and local titles at this
bookshop owned by local author Steve Brewer.
111 Carlisle Blvd. SE, (505) 553-3823, organicbooks.net

Retail Therapy ABQ
Owned by a mother–daughter duo, this shop
stocks brands that give back to philanthropic causes
and clothing and accessories bursting with local pride.
107 Amherst Dr. SE, (505) 219-3761, retailtherapyabq.com

FLIP OPEN
RED PLANET BOOKS & COMICS

This is one of only a handful of bookstores in North America devoted to titles by Native American authors. It becomes one of a kind with its focus on comics, games, and action figures by indigenous artists. In the store, you'll find children's books from authors like Sherman Alexie and Native American comic books like the well-known *Tribal Force* and *Super Indian*. It's the creation of Native Realities, a media company founded in Albuquerque that publishes and distributes Native American comic books. You'll find the company's own publications, too, like a comic book anthology and a collection celebrating World War II code talkers. (Code talkers, primarily Navajo tribal members from Arizona and New Mexico, created an unbreakable code in their language that helped the US gain the upper hand in the war.) The store highlights the amazing work of Native and indigenous artists in pop culture.

1002 Park Ave. SW, (505) 361-1182, redplanetbooksncomics.com

Neighborhood: Downtown, *Kid Friendly

TIP

The store doubles as the headquarters for IndigiPopX, originally Indigenous Comic Con. Founded in 2016, the convention celebrates Native Americans' contributions to comic books, superhero movies, and science fiction with panels, signings, and costume contests. indigipopx.com

ATTEND A LITERARY EVENT
AT BOOKWORKS

This locally owned indie bookstore has a calendar socialites would envy. It hosts numerous events annually. In 1984, founder Nancy Rutland opened the bookstore with the aim of creating a literary meeting place. New owners Danielle Foster and Wyatt Wegrzyn, both longtime employees, took over the business in 2011. Since then, they've expanded the store's presence as a "third place"—a locale between work and home for like-minded people to meet and discuss not only literature but also current events and social issues. Its monthly lineup includes author readings and talks, especially with writers of color or those who have traditionally been at the margins, as well as book club meetings and writing workshops. In addition to stocking new and used books by national authors, it shelves a hearty helping of titles by New Mexico and Southwest writers of every genre.

4022 Rio Grande Blvd. NW, (505) 344-8139, bkwrks.com

Neighborhood: North Valley, *Kid Friendly (depending on the author)

ACTIVITIES
BY SEASON

SPRING

SUMMER

FALL

WINTER

Jemez Hot Springs

SUGGESTED
ITINERARIES

ART LOVERS

Browse the National Hispanic Cultural Center, 76

Discover Secret Gallery, 109

Explore the University of New Mexico Art Museum, 92

Gallery Hop at Albuquerque Artwalk, 79

Peruse 516 ARTS, 104

Run Away to the OT Circus, 86

Browse the Tamarind Institute, 112

See an Exhibition at Harwood Art Center, 91

Browse the South Broadway Cultural Center, 90

Take a Public Art Walk, 83

Time Travel at Albuquerque Museum, 94

BOTTOMS UP

Pedal to Local Breweries, 31

Sip a Margarita at Sixty-Six Acres, 7

Toast the City from Level 5, 17

Sip Bubbly from Gruet, 14

CULTURE SEEKERS

DATE NIGHT

• •

FAMILIES

• •

GIRLS' DAY OR NIGHT OUT

MUSIC MAVENS

• •

GREAT OUTDOORS

LOCAVORES

THEATER GOERS

• •

Petroglyph National Monument

INDEX

• •

• •